Zen Wise Selling

ZenWise Selling

Mindful Methods
to Improve Your Sales ...
and Your Self

Lee Godden

Telsius
Publishing

Published by Telsius Publishing LLC
(Two Circles Press imprint), 2021 Obispo Avenue,
Signal Hill, California 90755 USA tel. (866) 936-9473
Visit the ZenWise website at www.zenwise.com.

Printed in the United States of America
Library of Congress Control Number: 2003096415
ISBN: 0-9740076-0-9
Cover design and photography by Lee Godden
Cover layout and graphics by RWR Marketing & Graphic Design

Publishers Cataloging in Publication
(Provided by Quality Books, Inc.)

Godden, Lee, 1958-
    ZenWise selling : mindful methods to improve your
sales-- and your self / Lee Godden. -- 1st ed.
    p. cm.
    Includes bibliographical references and index.
    LCCN 2003096415
    ISBN 0-9740076-0-9
    1. Selling 2. Business ethics 3. Business--
Religious aspects--Zen Buddhism 4. Meditations.
I. Title
HF5438.25.G64 2003   658.85
                    QBI03-700613

FIRST EDITION

For Rachel, my love and my best friend;

And for my father, T.W. Godden III, who was there for me;

And for my mother, Catherine, who followed her dreams;

And for my big brother, Terry, who is the ultimate role model.

CONTENTS AT A GLANCE

DETAILED TABLE OF CONTENTS

PREFACE

How many salespeople use the wisdom of Zen in their professional and personal life? Probably more than you think. Many people practice Zen without even knowing it!

It could be the salesperson whose energy seems to light up a room as they enter. Or the one whose calmness and confidence puts everyone around them at ease. It could be the person who sees their own challenges and failures as fantastic opportunities to learn. Or the salesperson who consistently closes more business than their peers, while seemingly unaffected by stress.

Interest in Zen is growing. Eastern thought has fascinated Westerners even before the transcendentalist musings of Emerson and Thoreau. Since it was first introduced to America a hundred years ago, Zen has seen a slow but steady adoption. Mass media and the Internet have helped Zen awareness surge in recent years. Most major cities have at least one Zen center.

Zen's message for salespeople is profound yet simple: practice business excellence by practicing personal excellence. Achieve fulfillment through awareness. Examine yourself closely and see how similar you are to—and how connected you are with—everyone around you. Instead of a *what's-in-it-for-me?* attitude, demonstrate compassion for your prospects, customers and coworkers. The result is a network of interpersonal bonds from which trust and communication flow effortlessly. Never forget that trust and communication are how products and services are sold.

Using Zen in sales, you assume nothing about who the customer is or what they want. You approach each new situation as a beginner would, even if you are an expert. Yet you are fully prepared. You immediately begin to establish credibility and value with the customer by educating them, following through on promises, then going the extra mile.

Applying Zen principles to both work and personal life can spur tremendous financial success. The most important benefit, however, is rediscovering simple things and ordinary moments. When you observe more, you experience more. Enjoy the journey. The destination is up to you.

ZenWise Selling breaks new ground by applying the ancient wisdom of Zen to the equally ancient profession of sales. This book is based on philosophical Zen, which has similarities to — but is different from — religious Zen Buddhism. Clergy of all faiths use Zen to deepen their connections with God, with their congregations and with themselves. Millions of others use Zen in their daily lives: construction workers, executives, teachers, lawyers and, yes, sales pros.

ZenWise Selling will help anyone involved in the sales process: sales reps, engineers, managers, executives, customers and buyers. If you are one of the thirteen million Americans employed as professional salespeople, *ZenWise Selling* will show you how to:

- Sell more, with less stress, using your unique selling style
- Experience in-the-moment joy while selling
- Communicate calmly and compassionately with customers
- Build strong, long-lasting customer relationships.

Zen's beauty is in the way it applies equally to both work and personal life. After reading this book you should be better able to:

- Truly understand yourself and what you desire
- See beauty in the ordinary
- Discover your connection with the world and everyone around you
- Be comfortable between extremes, in Zen's *middle way.*

This book focuses on the inner salesperson, and how to build mutually satisfying relationships with customers, peers, managers and subordinates. *ZenWise Selling* is designed to complement—not to replace—other books and training methodologies that address selling techniques.

ZenWise Selling takes you through each step of the selling process, including prospecting, customer relationship-building, presenting, team selling and managing salespeople. You'll learn about special meditations for salespeople that will help you achieve crystal clear focus on important tasks, by minimizing the brain's constant chatter.

You'll be presented with introspective list exercises that extract—and cause you to examine—your personal values, experiences, biases and goals. You can't know and respect your customer until you know and respect yourself. When that occurs, long-term customer relationships will develop and flourish.

Improving your sales as you improve your *self* at the same time...that's *ZenWise Selling*. You'll be amazed at what you discover.

Lee Godden is a longtime Zen practitioner, a trainer of corporate sales teams, and a speaker at business conferences worldwide. He is a former sales executive with Compaq and other Fortune companies. He lives in Signal Hill, California.

Visit www.zenwise.com for more information.

"We shall describe conditions of the soul that words can only hint at. We shall have to use logic to try to corner perspectives that laugh at our attempt."
- Huston Smith

AUTHOR'S NOTE TO THE READER

There's a Dilbert cartoon that illustrates the contempt most people have for salespeople:

- Salesman to Dilbert: *"Our new version is a step backward in quality and reliability. We're counting on your irrational need to have the latest version of every software product."*

- Dilbert to Salesman: *"I hate your weasel guts but I'll take one for home and one for the office."*

Over the last twenty-four years I've been a salesperson, a sales director and a Zen practitioner. During that time I don't think the public's perception about salespeople has changed much. Despite providing valuable products and services to practically everyone, salespeople are still mistrusted, lampooned and occasionally hated. Consider the stress and lack of self-esteem felt by the fictional Dilbert cartoon salesman. Consider how he often over-compensates for those feelings through arrogance and self-centeredness. Of course, it's only a cartoon, but sometimes fiction imitates life uncomfortably well.

I don't have to tell you that selling is becoming more difficult. Quotas are up, and the pressure is higher than ever. Yet approaching sales with a Zen mind has always helped me to stay focused, stay connected and stay balanced. My income has consistently been in the top five percent of sales professionals, and my accomplishments have never required contradicting my principles.

Personal success using Zen is more common than you may think. Interest in applying Eastern approaches to Western business continues to grow. To underscore this trend, a 2001 study published in the *American Journal of Health Promotion* demonstrated that stressed-out volunteers experienced an average 54% reduction in psychological distress after participating in a mindfulness training program that taught meditation skills.

శ్రీ   శ్రీ   శ్రీ

The idea for *ZenWise Selling* began when a business associate, seeing my work habits, asked me if there was a book on blending Zen into the busy, stressful life of a salesperson. I searched bookstores and the Internet for an *inner salesperson* guide, but nothing captured my outlook.

I found dozens of books on Zen, and even more on selling, but not one that combined both. Why wasn't there a book that spoke to the hearts—not just the minds—of salespeople and sales managers...a book that outlined specific steps to achieve greater spiritual and financial success simultaneously?

I was convinced at that point that I wanted to write such a book, because Zen's wisdom had helped me overcome many challenges, both business and personal. Sharing what I'd discovered as a *Zen-wise* sales professional seemed like a natural step.

The writing part came easily for me. Over the years I'd written and published about thirty magazine articles on business, technology and sports. But I quickly discovered that writing a book about applying Zen philosophy to sales was no small task.

Spurred by the love and encouragement from my family, friends and colleagues, I gathered and organized countless notes on Zen and sales. Early drafts of the book were critiqued by other authors, high-level sales executives and trusted advisors. I listened closely to their advice. The new book, *ZenWise Selling: Mindful Methods to Improve Your Sales and Your Self,* began to take shape.

I appreciated the life-is-constant-change wisdom of *Who Moved My Cheese?* and the practical advice of *The 7 Habits of Highly Effective People*. I wanted the tone of both of those books to be heard in *ZenWise Selling*. I also wanted to stress the application of philosophical Zen, rather than Zen Buddhism, to avoid possibly alienating those faithful to a particular religion.

An author needs to establish a voice in a book, and I decided early on not to write in an autobiographical, stories-of-my-success style. Instead I took a guide book approach, using each step in the selling process—customer care, prospecting, presenting, managing and team selling—as the framework for the chapters. After a year of writing, editing and rewriting, the book was completed.

ം   ം   ം

The goal of *ZenWise Selling* is to merge an increased inner and outer awareness into the conventional sales mindset. I encourage you to regularly examine your values, desires and strengths. My central message is that salespeople who understand themselves well, who strive to be experts in their field, and who act in accordance with their values, are seen by customers as compassionate, helpful and ethical...in other words, the type of salesperson with whom most customers prefer to do business.

After reading this book, send me an email at lee@zenwise.com and let me know if you think that this goal was accomplished. I've always appreciated honest feedback.

ॐ   ॐ   ॐ

Many friends, family members and colleagues played a key part in the creation of this book, but the project could not have been completed without the help of the following core group. These authors, sales executives and experts in Zen read and critiqued the manuscript through its development.

Specifically, I'd like to thank: Dr. Rachel Gilligan, my life partner and radiant source of encouragement; Harry Silverglide, the former vice president of sales for Extreme Networks, and an executive who demonstrates how interpersonal connections can be formed anywhere, at any time; David Ahee, the vice president of sales for ThinkEngine, and someone who practices the highest level of ethical salesmanship and leadership; Leslie Des Georges, the director of strategic sales for EMC, and a woman who is a shining example of balance between commitment to business excellence and maintaining a strong family life; Dr. Ronald Jue, co-author of *The Inner Edge* (McGraw-Hill, 2002), management consultant and early advisor to my *ZenWise Selling* efforts; Jeffrey Klein, Clio-award winning writer and talented music composer; Jane Gallagher, friend and spiritual lighthouse to many.

INTRODUCTION

What You Will Learn from *ZenWise Selling*

The best feeling in sales is when you don't need to employ high-pressure or tricky closing techniques because the customer emotionally agreed to buy soon after you established a mutual bond. Bonds with customers form when:

- You live and work according to an ethics-based personal value system
- You have in-depth knowledge of the customer's business, industry, problems, needs and biases
- You quickly establish credibility through clear communication and valuable education
- You demonstrate genuine, selfless compassion for the customer
- You earn the customer's trust and business by reliably delivering what you promise — then going the extra mile — during each step of the sales cycle.

Applying Zen philosophy to selling has two primary benefits:

1) You will sell more because of your ability to:
- Listen intently while the customer is speaking, and not tune them out to mentally compose your next statement
- Uncover the customer's business problems that need solving
- Allow your unique selling style to shine through while speaking and presenting
- Work in synchronicity with peers, managers and subordinates
- Reduce stress, calm yourself and re-focus before, during and after a hectic day of selling.

2) You will experience greater fulfillment at work and at home because of your ability to:
- Understand and honor yourself
- Feel compassion and respect for others
- Enjoy simplicity
- Live in-the-moment
- Find a balance and a connection with the world around you.

A word of caution. This book will be of little value to salespeople who:
- Choose to sell only once to each customer, with no interest in repeat business
- See little value in referrals to new prospects from satisfied customers
- Consider selling as a money-making exercise only
- Have no desire to look deeply inside themselves.

What is Zen?

Zen can be defined in several ways:

- A human science that deals with the mind

- An approach to living through in-the-moment awareness and compassion

- A philosophy, or a way of thinking.

Zen's aim is *practical living through relaxed examination of your inner self*. Zen, the philosophy, is not synonymous with Zen Buddhism, the religion. Modern Zen has roots in Indian Buddhism, Chinese Taoism and Ch'an, and Japanese Zen. *Appendix A: The Story Behind Zen* goes into more detail about Zen's history.

Zen's emphasis is on the internal, not the external. Deities and gods are not the focus, yet such beliefs are not excluded. A number of priests, pastors, ministers and rabbis are also active Zen practitioners. Zen's calm introspection enhances their spirituality by enabling deeper prayer.

Most of the millions who apply Zen to their daily life live in a house, not a monastery or a church. They wear casual clothes, business suits and uniforms, not robes. They are doctors, truck drivers, lawyers, students, construction workers and sales professionals. Each individual's outlook and spirituality is refreshingly unique.

Why Zen and Sales?

The elements that define selling—communication with others, dealing with deadlines, quotas, conflict resolution, rejection, fear and self-doubt—all provide fertile ground in which you can grow, and get to know yourself better. Self-knowledge leads to self-improvement, which opens the door to experiencing greater happiness and the ability to help others.

The marriage of Zen and sales involves harmoniously connecting the values you apply in your personal life with the values you apply in your work life. Such a bond is often missing or is inconsistently joined.

Ask yourself two questions:

1) What are my true values?
2) Do I leave those values at home when I go to work, or are they infused into everything I say and do throughout the day?

What you value defines who you are...your true nature. Reflecting on your true nature, and living in accordance with what you discover, leads to increased awareness. Awareness is sometimes called wakefulness. This doesn't mean sleeping fewer hours. It means spending your waking hours performing thoughts and actions that are less *auto-pilot*, and more *hands-on flying*. Practice wakefulness for awhile and you'll see an increase in your overall awareness of the world and of the humanity around you. You may become quite amazed at the beauty, intricacy and *connectedness* of everything. Wakefulness leads some to shake their heads in awe, others to laugh with joy, and others to cry tears of thanks.

Lessons from a Zen Sage

"In Zen there is always the feeling that awakening is something quite natural, something startlingly obvious, which may occur at any moment . . ."
Alan Watts[1]

Being fully aware and awake is experiencing what some call enlightenment. Enlightenment is neither magical nor mystical, although it is essentially impossible to describe with mere words. Description isn't really necessary, however, because you were born enlightened.

As a child you often behaved with the creativity and spontaneity of enlightenment. As a youth you were told to think and behave in pre-defined ways. You probably rebelled at first, sensing the pitfalls of rigidity. As an adult, making money, starting a family and collecting possessions became the goal, even though you may still rebel in certain ways. Despite the ways you've changed, you've never relinquished your enlightenment. You may have simply placed it in your emotional attic, as a curious object to be dusted off some time in the future.

There's no time like now to look deeply and to experience fully. In fact, there's no time except now.

Why Do Salespeople Need a Personal Philosophy?

The traits of successful salespeople were uncovered through extensive surveys conducted during the writing of the book, *Coaching Champions: How to Get the Absolute Best Out of Your Salespeople*.[2] Authors Salisbury, Neary and O'Connor found that successful salespeople:

- Have a purpose in life
- Display more self-knowledge
- Display more respect for the customer
- Use low-pressure — not high-pressure — selling techniques
- Accept personal responsibility for their successes and failures
- Know that continued success requires helping others get what they want.

These traits paint a picture of a calm, confident, compassionate salesperson. For some, calmness is not an element of the selling process, but instead something to look forward to when the day is over. Calmness after a hectic day of selling may involve family, friends, spiritual work, physical activities, reading, relaxing, eating, drinking, or a little of each.

Why not make calmness an elemental part of selling? If it's part of your personal philosophy, calmness can be applied when you win and when you lose, when you're on top of the world, and when nothing seems to be going right. Calmness aids clarity. A philosophy of calmness keeps things in balance, and minimizes wild swings back and forth between elation and despair. Losses are no longer automatic triggers for sadness. Wins are merely the sweet fruit of your labor.

Throughout the ages, philosophers ranging from Socrates to Sartre have analyzed their worlds and taught ways of placing thoughts, actions and consequences into a reasonable context. Some philosophers focused on religion, some questioned God. Some championed democracy, some taught communism. Some challenged the conventional wisdom of their time, and some paid for their words with their lives. (The author hopes this book won't be nearly as controversial.)

In contrast to the current emphasis on fast food and instant gratification, philosophy's answers to life's questions, problems and crises don't come in convenient nugget form. Applying reason to any complex system requires patient study. Developing new techniques and habits requires self-discipline.

Words from the Wise

"Humankind's basic trend toward spiritual growth is the perennial philosophy."
Aldous Huxley

Philosophy is enjoying an increase in popularity. As the world seemingly spins faster and faster, many are demanding that it slow down so they can enjoy the view for awhile. Modern philosophers such as Jurgen Habermas are teaching new ways to interpret and understand communication styles, moral consciousness, and metaphysical thinking.

A particular philosophy is easily accepted and understood when it blends well with other viewpoints. Such is Zen. Without its own religious dogma, rites and rituals, codes and commandments, Zen sits well in the same room with those who value such things, and with those who don't. Embracing diversity is a Zen tenet.

Any philosophy that helps people come to terms with the modern world is worthy of the time it takes to understand its logic, precepts and conclusions. The human mind—along with the thoughts, emotions and actions it produces—is a powerful tool. And keeping tools sharp ensures years of usefulness and enjoyment.

About the Meditations in This Book

At first glance, the addition of meditation to the already-busy life of a salesperson may seem counterproductive. It's easy to conjure up a comical image of a roomful of business-suited professionals, sitting cross-legged on mats and chanting, "Omm," instead of making phone calls and closing deals.

A more realistic and representative image, however, is of the same professionals making phone calls and closing deals in a highly productive and focused manner as a result of the snippets of time they've taken before and during the day to reflect, to re-center and to re-energize themselves.

Meditation is the deliberate slowing down of your thoughts to calm yourself inside and out, which in turn allows your natural awareness to emerge. When meditation relaxes the mind, priorities come into clear focus. Solutions appear faster in an uncluttered brain.

All sorts of people—customers, CEOs, politicians, soldiers—are blending meditative practices into their daily lives. Zen teaches that the introspection gained from meditation allows compassion to grow. A mindset of *How can I help others?* makes a fundamental difference in the business world of selling and buying. Person-to-person connections are made stronger, while passing moments are enjoyed more fully.

Such mindfulness is your birthright.

A world without calm, peaceful mindfulness is a world of slavery…slavery to an overactive mind on auto-pilot, generating millions of repetitious, mindless actions and reactions. A mind on auto-pilot leaves you—the true pilot—to sleepwalk through life, doing things the way you've always done them.

The Zen way to cultivate a calm, creative mind is to take a few minutes several times each day to pause, to breath slowly, to slow down the thoughts, and to reflect. The idea of meditation may spur some salespeople to cry, "I can't afford to lose precious selling minutes!" After one or two meditations, however, the same salespeople realize that it's time well spent.

Words from the Wise

"Your brain shall be your servant instead of your master. You will rule it instead of allowing it to rule you."
  Charles E. Popplestone

Perspectives often change during a hectic day. What started out in the morning as a grand plan for accomplishment and success sometimes shatters into a random collection of interruptions, phone calls, emails, impromptu meetings, social chats and diversions. Stopping the procession of activity, and slowing the procession of thoughts in your mind, for just a few minutes, helps you regain your initial perspective and allow your innate wisdom to re-emerge.

Suggested meditations are included throughout *ZenWise Selling*. Take a break from reading and try them out and as you come across them, or wait until you're in a comfortable, private place later on. Don't forget to try each meditation at least once, though. The first time through it may feel odd. "What am I doing?" you may think. "I'm just sitting here, breathing. What's the big deal?" The goal of meditation is to quiet that constant brain chatter and to enable an intimate connection with the inner you. Experimenting with various forms of meditation will reveal what works well for you, and what doesn't. Over time you'll develop a personalized meditation style and routine that is calming and helpful.

About the List Exercises in This Book

As you encounter them, take a few minutes to complete the list exercises in this book. The exercises focus on your personal feelings, beliefs and experiences as a salesperson. List exercises are a form of guided journal writing. Self-knowledge is key in self-improvement.

The effect of completing a list exercise will range from merely interesting to entirely therapeutic. What you write down is who you are, today. There are no right or wrong answers. Go back at a later date and reflect upon what you wrote. Consider how your personal, unique selling style has changed.

The first few answers to a particular list exercise may come quickly. For example, the exercise, "List your best moments in sales," may initially cause you to write down your most financially rewarding wins. As you dig deeper you may remember the sale in which you learned a valuable lesson about human behavior, the meeting in which you met an inspiring person, or the customer who thanked you for solving a huge problem, even though the sale itself was small.

Write down as many or as few answers as you prefer. The exercises aren't tests, they are self-discovery.

It's Your Journey

Life is a journey during which each moment, each mile traveled, is either savored or overlooked. For many the focus is on vague future destinations—money, possessions, success, retirement—instead of what's happening in-the-moment. Trading the experience of right now for thoughts about the future is generally a poor deal.

After reading about new approaches to life and selling, the next step is to experience them. Practice introspection, calmness, and compassion during a tough day at the office, then examine how you feel after work. What worked? What didn't? Which methods need more refinement?

With a well-functioning value system and a personalized philosophy toward life and work, each day becomes more authentic, more comprehensible, and more full. What you believe in, and what you value, will begin to appear.

Look closely at yourself...your values, your desires and your strengths. What you see may fascinate you. It may scare you too. That's okay. A life spent looking outward for insight makes introspection uncomfortable at first.

Introduction

Salespeople who understand themselves well, and who live in accordance with their values, tend to attract others to them. Customers see such salespeople as reliable, trustworthy, good listeners who selflessly give extra effort...in other words, the kind of salesperson with whom they prefer to do business.

Some may be tempted to skim through the material looking for quick tips and tricks to make more money, while ignoring "all of that Zen stuff." Sorry, it doesn't work that way. Zen principles—such as compassion for others and in-the-moment living—can't be punched in and out like a time clock. They are either part of you, or they are not.

So get ready to see some new ways of looking at the career path you have chosen. The journey you're experiencing is the result of conscious choices you've made in the past. What new choices will you make today? *ZenWise Selling* is a book, yet you must do more than read. Reading about the Grand Canyon doesn't compare to standing on the rim and having your breath taken away by the grand vista.

1
THE CHALLENGES OF SELLING

Where Salespeople Come From

Thirteen million people are employed as professional, full-time salespeople in the United States. Few of them, early in life, chose sales as a career. Most were educated or specialized in a field in which they saw salespeople in action. "Hey!" they said. "I could do that!"

Many of these enterprising folk saw the money that salespeople make, or the freedom they enjoy. Maybe it was the attraction of interacting with different people each day, or of visiting different places. For some it was the lure of the unknown, the risk of living with commission being a large part (sometimes the only part) of their compensation. Some picked sales because they wanted to make a positive difference in their lives, and in the lives of others.

There's a certain wildness, an uncertainty, to selling that is attractive, and sometimes intoxicating. Adrenaline junkies, risk takers and Type-A personalities are drawn to selling's who-knows-what-will-happen-next lifestyle. Such *adventure capitalists* will thrive in sales as long as they can skillfully handle the flip side of Wow! — namely rejection, frustration and loss.

The notion that most salespeople fall into their occupation is even more remarkable when considering that sellers impact the lives of practically everyone. Selling is done by humans, to humans. Emotions ranging from bliss to anger have always been part of the selling process, in both buyer and seller. Sales is a vocation, it is what someone does. It is often a large part their identity.

Selling is an old profession. From the food and fabric merchants of ancient Greece and China to today's globally connected, high-tech sales pros, the art of guiding buyers toward purchasing goods and services has come a long way.

Science and technology have put modern day sellers on a fast-moving treadmill. Missing bids, proposal deadlines and other opportunities by mere hours or minutes can turn a sale into a loss...a commission check that buys a vacation into one that barely buys the groceries.

The prerequisites for entry into the profession of sales are minimal and inconsistent. The level of education required varies, and a widely acknowledged credential or certification is lacking, although Sales and Marketing Executives International offers designations such as Certified Sales Executive (CSE©) to properly trained and qualified individuals.

Typically, the hiring process is something like: "Can you learn about these products? Can you make phone calls? Can you speak convincingly with customers? Can you close? Great! Can you start now?"

Although sales is easy to enter, it is a difficult career in which to consistently do well. Some salespeople make $30,000 a year. Some make well over $300,000. Higher incomes often fluctuate wildly from month to month, and year to year.

Sales is also a tough profession to feel good about. Sharp, stinging opinions are often expressed about salespeople, both in general and by name. Compliments are heard, but the majority of words directed at or about salespeople are negative.

Exercise#1: List the jobs and life events that preceded you becoming a salesperson

- _____
- _____
- _____
- _____
- _____

How Salespeople are Viewed by Customers

Lawyer jokes notwithstanding, salespeople are some of the most misunderstood and maligned folks on the planet. The rancor—based on poor experiences with salespeople, or experiences with poor salespeople—includes colorful descriptions such as slimy, money-hungry and self-absorbed.

Worth a Smile
"There are worse things in life than death. Have you ever spent an evening with an insurance salesman?"
Woody Allen

Yet examined individually, a salesperson is no more dishonest than the average person. They are, in fact, average people, trying to make a living the best way possible, trying to do well, and trying to do good.

A problem that plagues many salespeople is viewing the customer as a target, a one-time deal, as opposed to a new relationship that can lead to repeat sales and referrals. An in-and-out, adversarial mindset sets the stage for stressful and non-productive business.

Customers often see slick, professional salespeople as machines. Salespeople describe themselves that way sometimes. "Did you hear about Jackson's latest win? She is a selling *machine!*"

Jackson is likely quite human. If she consistently sells more than the rest of the sales team, she probably understands her personal values and ethics well, she connects with prospects and customers on an emotional level, and she considers each customer a unique relationship to be developed, instead of another target to be conquered.

Help Wanted: Must be Able to Smile Under Stress

The sales process can be defined as: *The art and skill of guiding customers to buy products and services via the salesperson's calm, proactive management of change and uncertainty.* This artful, skillful guidance requires:

☺ Knowledge of your company's products and services
☺ Knowledge of the steps and mechanics of the sales process
☺ Knowledge of the customer's needs, desires and biases
☺ Trustworthiness and reliability
☺ Friendly, helpful, energetic attitude
☺ Self-confidence.

Unfortunately, sales has other, not so nice, requirements, such as the ability to:

☹ Put up with customer resistance and rejection on a regular basis
☹ Strive for a sales quota that can seem at best doable, and at worst impossible
☹ Deal with sales managers and coworkers who are under intense pressure from their management
☹ Struggle with your own company's problems in areas such as quality, support, shipping, and billing
☹ Stay awake for tedious sales review meetings, alternating between extreme boredom (when other salespeople are presenting their sales plan to management) and extreme anxiety (when it's your turn)

☹ Accept the uncertain lifestyle that sales offers. King-of-the-hill one month. What-have-you-done-for-me-lately? the next.

If you've been in sales awhile, you may be nodding your head at this point. All jobs have ups and downs, good and bad aspects. Anyone can become a salesperson, but the ones who are consistently successful are the best at handling constant change.

Exercise #2: List the occupations you'd consider if you weren't a salesperson

- _____
- _____
- _____
- _____
- _____

Change and Uncertainty: the Essence of Sales

When asked to boil down his outlook on life into a simple phrase, distinguished Zen master Shunryu Suzuki replied, "Everything changes."[3] Zen offers simple ways to deal with change, both personally and professionally. Many people resist change. The Zen way is to embrace it. Fighting change expends energy, and such a battle is seldom winnable. Depleted and exhausted, the _change fighter_ finds little enjoyment in the present moment, and focuses instead on future happiness.

Selling effectively demands nimble adjustment to newness. When your company changes the product you're selling or changes the message the customer will hear, why waste time being surprised or frustrated? Agile, responsive companies thrive. Such corporate agility means the sales force will be required to juggle an ever-changing array of balls in the air. Sometimes they'll have to replace the balls with an entirely new set. Sometimes they'll have to learn an entirely new way to juggle!

Chapter 1: The Challenges of Selling

The ever-changing lifestyle of a salesperson can be dealt with in two ways: fight it, or accept it. If you hate selling, hate your company, constantly complain about your boss or your customers, or if you're essentially a full-time grouch, you may want to consider other career options.

Even if you love sales it's easy to find yourself stymied by the constant ups and downs, plusses and minuses, good times and bad. Dealing with the turbulence of sales requires personal introspection involving understanding, acceptance and continuous self-improvement. Customers, companies, managers and coworkers will forever be as unpredictable as the wind. Change is constant. Success and failure are impermanent.

Bad Things Happen to Stressed Salespeople

Few occupations are free of stress, and sales is no exception. Stress in sales comes from:

- Customer deadlines and management expectations.
- Quotas and the need to close deals
- Finding new prospects while handling existing customer needs
- Competitive pressure and peer pressure.

Salespeople who have a substantial personal financial debt and large monthly car and house payments are under an extra load of stress. Toss in one or two personal issues – perhaps involving spouses, children or parents – and the stress needle goes into the red zone.

Humans are wired for dealing with stress. Early man drew on stress and the connected fight-or-flight response to find food, build shelter and avoid being mauled by wild animals. How stress is handled, not stress itself, is the issue. Most doctors agree that dealing poorly with stress creates health problems.

> ## Something to Consider
> Sales may seem like the most stressful occupation, but it isn't. Consider soldiers under fire, air traffic controllers, police officers approaching a suspicious vehicle, trauma surgeons, and convenience store cashiers working at 2 a.m., alone. Consider Peace Corps volunteers working in war-torn regions. Consider single moms juggling sick babies and a demanding boss. Now that's stress! All in all, sales pros have it pretty good.

A simplistic way to deal with stress is to avoid it. But constantly trying to stay out of harm's way is tiptoeing through life. You'll arrive safely at death, with little to say about the experience of living. In place of avoidance, seek to examine the way you internalize emotions and externalize blame when things go stressfully wrong.

Stress in salespeople can be seen in various ways. Salespeople who are poor listeners are often stressed. So too are those who are regularly late for appointments, and those who constantly criticize others.

Salespeople who anger quickly are often stressed. Objectively examined after cooling down, anger is a wonderful tool for seeing personal triggers and emotional pressure points. Although a solution may not be immediately evident, looking at the reasons behind the anger can be a catalyst for change.

Some salespeople see their stress as a badge of honor. To anyone who'll listen they proudly proclaim the number of hours they've worked ("56 hours last week!"), the sleep they've missed, and the vacation they haven't taken in years. These statements are actually badges of sorrow, not honor. "Look at my sacrifice and admire it!" is the true message. In the spirit of *oneupmanship*, will the next sad mark of distinction be to brag about a divorce or a heart attack caused by work stress?

Such pain bragging defines happiness as something good to be enjoyed some other time, but not in the present moment. Identifying oneself primarily through the lack of a personal life and an overbearing workload begs the question: does such an outlook end mercifully only with death, perhaps preceded by a brief retirement?

Something to Consider

The next time a coworker brags about never having time to eat, invite the poor soul out to a nice business lunch. Keep the conversation off work topics. Insist they have dessert. They deserve it.

Besides the physical and emotional consequences of stress, spiritual deficit often occurs too. Compassion, that tender human ability, is often lost in a cloud of stress. The loss of compassion may begin with seemingly insignificant compromises. Later it may progress into a gradual withdrawal from work, friends and family. The ultimate loss of natural compassion is a cold, emotionless view of human connections as a waste of time and energy. The statement, "If it doesn't have a way of making me money, I'm not interested in doing it," is often said in jest, but the underlying emotion may be quite ominous.

When income rises, balance is at risk. Living at the upper end of a lifestyle that depends on an uncertain or barely sustainable income is like wearing golden handcuffs. Your alternatives are limited and you feel trapped. When your only option is to work as hard as possible and hope that your income level doesn't drop, debilitating stress creeps into picture, making life even tougher.

Stressful situations are an integral part of selling. The question is, how do you deal with stress when it occurs?

A 2001 study published in the *American Journal of Health Promotion* demonstrated that stressed-out participants experienced an average 54% reduction in psychological distress after completing a mindfulness training program that taught meditation skills. While prior studies showed patients with confirmed psychiatric illness improved with meditation, the newer study showed that the general population greatly benefits too. The study involved a mindfulness training program (28 hours over 8 weeks) that included meditation, yoga and stress-reduction techniques, plus an 8-hour retreat. The improvements were essentially unchanged three months after the conclusion of the study.[4]

Signs of Sales Burn-Out

A jet engine burns out when it depletes its fuel. When a sales-person has expended their last drop of energy into selling, and the results are less than expected, *sales burnout* occurs. Some indicators of sales burn-out include the following problematic feelings and behaviors:

- Organizational disorder (office always a mess); forgetfulness or absentmindedness; lack of creativity
- Laziness or procrastination; looking busy when you're not; boredom; lack of energy
- Lying or exaggeration to avoid confrontation; impulsive deviations from daily tasks
- Regular daydreaming, fantasizing or scattered thoughts; focus on the past or the future; constant worry
- Complaining, cynicism and sarcasm; no sense of humor; inability to receive criticism; resentment of others; abuse of power (for managers)
- Discomfort being alone (always being with others); isolation from others
- Eating or drinking too much; inability to sleep well; regular colds or flu
- Perfectionism; excessive focus on looks or body; constant approval-seeking
- Depression or profound sadness about job and life; self-doubt of own abilities; hopelessness.

It's normal for everyone to experience some of these problems from time to time. When they begin to dominate your experiences, it's time to examine the causes. Zen is neither a cure for these problems nor a substitute for professional psychological counseling. If you regularly identify with more than two or three of the above signs, you may benefit from examining your philosophies — or lack thereof — about selling. What is important to you? What do you value?

Exercise #3: List the most frustrating aspects of selling

- _____
- _____
- _____
- _____
- _____

The Mindful Salesperson

The hallmarks of mindfulness include:

- Your professional desires and goals are in accordance with your personal values
- You communicate with — and treat — others in accordance with your personal values
- Your expectations of others are in line with their abilities, uniqueness and freedom of choice
- You accept fear and failure as necessary components of personal growth, in both yourself and others.

Most salespeople have a large, untapped pool of creativity, wisdom, compassion and personal power. Unfortunately, this pool of positive attributes sometimes remains eternally trapped, frozen under a sheet of conventional ways of dealing with challenges and opportunities. To crack the ice requires strength, but the return on invested effort can be life changing.

Doing nothing to tap into your true nature is understandable yet regrettable. The pressures of family, health, bills, traffic, bosses, customers, deadlines and quotas make it tough to eke out even a few moments each day for rest and relaxation, not to mention working on complex issues such as values, philosophies and personal growth.

To use a baseball analogy, the trick isn't in eliminating life's curve balls. You can't control what the pitcher—or life—throws at you. The trick is to see each pitch through crystal clear eyes, and to develop, through disciplined practice, skills that enable you to quickly, calmly and confidently choose if and how you're going to swing in response.

"*If I were to begin life again, I should want it as it was. I would only open my eyes a little more.*"
- Jules Renard

2

TO KNOW YOURSELF IS TO KNOW THE CUSTOMER

Define Success for Yourself

Sales is a wonderful profession that enables people of diverse interests and backgrounds to achieve what many only dream of. The money can be good, but wealth and happiness are not synonymous. Money buys goods and services, not emotional and spiritual fulfillment.

Exercise #4: What is Success to You?

Success in sales is defined differently, depending on what you value. Here are some varied outcomes of success. How would you rank them in order of importance?

Rank	Achievement
____	Money
____	Career advancement
____	Knowledge or wisdom
____	Education or certification
____	Mastery of technical or selling techniques
____	Time with family and friends
____	Enjoyment of solitude, peace and quiet
____	Progress toward a religious goal/spiritual path
____	_____ (add your own)
____	_____ (add your own)

The rankings you choose are neither right nor wrong, merely a discovery of what you value. What you value may change over time. Your success can be judged by how well you achieve what you consider important. Conversely, when you know what you value, yet you consciously neglect to act in accordance with those values, you will be conflicted. Society's commonly used portrayals of success may be different from yours. Creatively develop your own definitions using your innate uniqueness as your guide.

What Do You Truly Desire?

A Zen tenet is that suffering is often caused by desire. When you don't get what you desire, you suffer.

Desire is not inherently bad, but failing to understand the motivations behind desire often results in a constant state of wanting more. When describing someone as, "desirous of large, incredible things," the first assumption is of expensive houses and fast cars. However, if that person's desire is focused on such goals as ending diseases, feeding the hungry, sheltering the homeless, protecting children, caring for animals or introducing helpful new technologies, then their desire is completely altruistic.

Desire for basics such as shelter, food and sleep are good, simply because without these things an organism will die. Desire for sex, notably for procreation, is also good. Celibacy has debatable merits for individuals, but a celibate civilization soon perishes.

Problems with desire occur when boredom and a lack of fulfillment lead into a repeating, never-ending cycle of experiencing sensations and of acquiring more and more. Many salespeople are focused on money alone...buying things that will enhance their self-image or give them an edge over others.

Something to Consider

Boredom is a tremendous self-help tool. In an effort to find mind-fulness, consider boredom a free ticket into a period of quiet stillness. Accept the boredom as a gift, and immerse completely into it. When bored, be as bored as you can possibly be. Let the emptiness guide your mind into enjoying the moment and enjoying the peace. Gradually allow aware thought to emerge.

Fast-paced culture makes slow-paced betterment tough to swallow. Even desire for spiritual enlightenment and religious attainment may cause suffering when such goals are not reached quickly enough

Take care in what you desire. Examine it, and accept it as sensible as long as your desire coincides with your personal values and basic needs, and is not harmful to others.

Is Desire for Money and Possessions Wrong?

Desire for money and possessions is not wrong if the desire is in balance with other non-financial elements in your life. The attraction of winning every deal, making tons of money, and living in the biggest house is strong. Yet the promise of the benefits of accumulation is often greater than the reality. Those who have accumulated luxury cars and big homes know that the need for a continuous stream of big paychecks may be more restraining than liberating.

Experiencing happiness without regard to an object's or an activity's financial value is the key. Sacrificing happiness today for a potentially happy future is antithetical to the definition of happiness. Happiness is joy right now, not joy in the dead past or the imaginary future. Trading the enjoyment of each moment in favor of a chance for future happiness means the destination is more important than the journey. The realization of the folly of such an outlook usually comes too late.

Words from the Wise
"Lives based on having are less free than lives based on doing or being."
E.Y. Harburg

By seeking Zen's *middle way* — the avoidance of extremes and the seeking of balance in viewpoints and actions — you experience delight during each moment of your work and life, while still working hard toward goals you've set. The meshing together of your work, your personal life, your goals and your values into the here-and-now is the experience of bliss.

The Drawbacks of Auto-Pilot

Flying on auto-pilot makes sense when the weather is clear and you're free from challenges for long stretches of time. Selling successfully is seldom accomplished in such a calm sky.

Some salespeople self-assuredly insist that they know their products and their customer base so well that they can, at a moment's notice, "...sell an icebox to an Eskimo." Another statement of overconfidence is, "I can sell this stuff in my sleep." It feels great to say such powerful things — and to bask in the glow of the awestruck listener — but it also speaks volumes about the salesperson's standardized, preset selling style and their possible lack of consideration for each unique customer.

Confidence acquired from years of success is a positive attribute for a salesperson. When previously successful techniques are applied too broadly to current customers, however, confidence degrades into a form of arrogance that actually limits the potential for success.

What will happen if you say, "As of right now, I know nothing about sales," to yourself? Just saying those words out loud can bring about a gut reaction. "No, that's not true! I've worked my whole career developing these skills." Still, consider the impact of such a statement.

You'd have to learn from scratch selling techniques, your products, your customers and your company. You'd have to look at situations and problems through fresh eyes, instead of through those of a dragon-slaying sales god.

Constant openness to new ideas, approaches and techniques is not as tough as it sounds. By knowing yourself, you know much about the emotional make-up of your customer. Every emotion you've ever felt—happiness, fear, anger, indifference, pride, distrust—has been experienced by each of your customers. The door for empathy, not just sympathy, is now wide open. In Zen, such *sameness* embodies a universal connection and compassion.

Words from the Wise

"The delusion of experiencing ourselves as different from the rest becomes a prison for us."
Albert Einstein

Acting on the intrinsic similarities between you and your customer forges a mutually satisfying and beneficial relationship. Conversely, highlighting differences begins a decaying process that separates viewpoints and injures relationships.

Cultivate Your Beginner's Mind

Zen teachings often refer to the *beginner's mind*. Another similar phrase is *not-knowing mind*. For those who have been selling for a long time, this is a particularly important lesson. Westerners often equate not knowing with amateurish behavior. The opposite is true. Experts in a particular subject who remain at the top of their game do so by approaching every situation as a one of a kind learning experience. They are alert and flexible to new ideas and methodologies.

Lessons from a Zen Sage
"If your mind is empty, it is always open to everything...In the beginner's mind there are many possibilities, but in the expert's mind there are few."
Shunryu Suzuki [5]

Beginner's mind, when used by a sales professional, is an opportunity for a deep connection with a customer. A difficult aspect of beginner's mind is shedding the been-there-done-that approach to any given sales situation. Knowing the tricks of the trade, including the arrogant and optimistic ability to "...read a customer like a book" does more to limit a sales experience than to expand it. As with judging books by their covers, the valuable content inside remains hidden under assumptions.

To cultivate a beginner's mind, start by acknowledging your desire to discover new ways of looking at yourself, your customers, and your profession. Such openness leads to a wider array of options, which leads to more chances for success.

Exercise #5: List the best things that have been said to/about you during your sales career:

- _____
- _____
- _____
- _____
- _____

No Battles, Just Diplomacy and Peacemaking

Some sales how-to texts compare sales techniques to those of battle. From full frontal assaults, to dividing and conquering, to employing ancient Chinese warring moves, fighting words have crept into the vernacular of sales. These methodologies contain useful strategies and tactics, yet problems occur when salespeople take battle analogies to heart.

The theory that the "soldier" (salesperson) is in a "fight" (sales effort) with the "enemy" (the competitor) results in the customer cast in two largely unwanted roles:

- Pre-fight battlefield
- Post-fight booty for the victorious "army" (sales organization) who employed superior "weaponry" (strategies and tactics).

Most customers want no part in other people's battles. They simply want to examine, test and possibly purchase the best product that fits their plans, problems and budget. It doesn't matter if the customer is looking at a million-dollar computer system, a five thousand-dollar used car, or a thirty-dollar per month gym membership, they just need help from knowledge-able, trustworthy salespeople who represent a company with excellent products and support.

War and battle are, unfortunately, still realities in the modern world. Being killed or wounded, or killing or wounding another, is often romanticized in novels and movies, but military veterans will attest to the real-life lack of romance involved. Hand-to-hand combat training focuses on enemy vulnerability points, mainly the eyes, throat and groin. The object is to immobilize or kill. Where is the analogy to selling?

Selling is an exercise in understanding when *not* to do battle. If you yearn to experience the sales warrior spirit, then adopt non-violent elements of the soldier's mindset, such as:

- Always be prepared to face a tough challenge
- Believe in your training, your abilities, and your righteousness
- Focus the mind on the desired outcome.

If you love a contest, challenge yourself to find new ways to unite your energy with that of your customer. Help the customer uncover and define unique problems that need solving, then work as hard as it takes to design and deliver creative solutions that fit those needs.

Selling with a Zen beginner's mind gives an advantage over those who use strictly standard approaches to solving problems. Display creativity with compassion and customers will take notice. When salespeople place their own needs on the back burner and focus primarily on helping the customer, the long-term results are rewarding for all parties.

Sometimes customers will encourage battle—in the form of price wars—between sales organizations vying for their business. If a customer wants such a battle, rest assured that you don't, for two reasons:

1. If the salesperson can't adequately convince the customer of any reason—besides price—to buy, then the salesperson must decide whether or not such a customer is worth the effort.

2. Customers who do business strictly on price have no loyalty to any sales organization. Repeat business and referrals are unlikely.

The Downside of Multitasking

The pride that many salespeople take in their ability to multi-task often creates more problems than it solves. Multitasking is appropriate when the second, or concurrent, activity takes nothing away from the first, or primary, activity. Driving is a good example. It's difficult to imagine driving a car without doing something else. (Motorcyclists tend to have a different viewpoint.) Without losing focus on the weighty responsibility of driving safely, it is generally considered safe to concurrently listen to the radio or to an audio book.

Problems arise when taking on activities, while driving, that defocus primary attention from the task at hand. Talking on the cell phone while driving is risky, but even more so is taking your eyes off the road to push cell phone buttons, jot down phone numbers, or look for a customer file in the back seat. It's well known that driver inattention frequently causes traffic accidents.

Applied to selling, when in front of a customer, pay the closest possible attention to everything the customer says and does. A strong temptation as the customer is talking is to nod your head and mutter "Uh-huh" while you're composing your next words. Unfortunately, your brilliant response may not have the desired outcome because you missed a key remark or a non-verbal gesture made by the customer.

Tuning out—even for a few seconds—the customer's comments and questions is placing a bet that what you're thinking about is more important than what the customer is saying.

Lessons from a Zen Sage

In this ancient Zen parable, a student is washing dirty bowls in the sink. The teacher asks what the student is thinking. The student says he is thinking about how wonderful a warm cup of tea will taste after the washing is finished. The teacher explains that this is poor Zen practice. *"When doing the dishes, do the dishes!"* the teacher admonishes. *"Feel the water running through your fingers, feel the texture of the brush, the smoothness of the bowls."* The student asks why looking forward to a simple cup of tea is harmful. *"Because,"* the teacher explains, *"while you are sipping the tea you will be thinking about how soft your pillow will feel when you finish the tea and go to bed. Learn to savor each moment for itself. When drinking tea, drink tea!"*

The practical benefits of single-tasking include:

- Efficient exchange of information
- Reduction of misunderstandings
- Creation of trust

- Openness for creative brainstorming between you and the customer.

Multitasking has downsides in other selling activities in addition to speaking with customers. Focusing on tasks such as prospecting, researching and reporting helps those tasks reach completion. Focusing also helps to tune out interruptions. The problems with incomplete tasks are:

- The act of restarting the task at a later time involves repetition of already-done sub-tasks that take even more time away from a crowded work schedule.

- The lack of a sense of accomplishment and of getting somewhere. Distracting thoughts of, "I have to finish that report!" take your focus away from other matters.

- Coworkers and management relying on your completion of the task become more stressed themselves. Beware of creating a reputation as one who can't be trusted to complete assigned tasks.

See *Chapter Ten: Advice on Successful, Mindful Selling* for more information on time management, interruption management and task prioritization.

Living and Selling In-The-Moment

Central to Zen is being *in-the-moment* as much as possible. This is more difficult than it seems. Simply pausing to breathe slowly and to clear the mind for as little as fifteen seconds will prompt the mind to generate past- and future-scenario thoughts, even when they are not desired.

As a salesperson, while listening to a customer speak, it's easy to tell when you are not in-the-moment. Your mind will wander and you will lose focus on the customer's words. Thoughts pop into your head: what you'll say next, the upcoming meeting with your manager, the sales forecast that is due, and what you'll be having for dinner.

It's essentially impossible to be in-the-moment all the time. The trick is to realize that your attention is wandering from the subject at hand, and then to gently guide it back into focus. Failure to notice that you're not in-the-moment, or noticing it but choosing to do nothing to correct it, will, over time, lead to other problems that reduce selling effectiveness:

- You'll lack self confidence in your ability to find, attract, close and retain customers.

- You'll develop poor working habits and communications skills.

- You'll enjoy sales less.

- You'll see your sales income decline, which in turn creates more self-defeating problems.

Meditation is an excellent way to increase your ability to stay in-the moment.

"Vitality shows not only in the ability to persist but in the ability to start over."
- F. Scott Fitzgerald

3
MEDITATION: THE CALM BEFORE THE SELL

Reasons to Meditate

Meditation allows mindfulness to develop, and customers prefer to do business with mindful salespeople. Customers like being clearly heard and fully understood. Mindful salespeople are remembered and respected by customers, and they are usually the ones called when the customer has a need. Mindful salespeople tend to:

- Pay closer attention to, and enjoy, the detail of the moment.

- Truly listen to customers and coworkers, and not half-listen while thinking about something else.

- See difficult customers and coworkers as lessons for growth, not irritating impediments.

- Enjoy the ups and downs of a typical day of selling, without grumbling or constantly looking forward to getting home to "finally enjoy what's left of the day."

Meditation is a wonderful way to begin — or to continue — your journey of self-discovery and awareness. Zen teaches that discovering your true values, your true self, your true essence, is a quest well worth the effort. Once discovered, your essence is tough to ignore. Everything you think, say and do—including making mistakes—is in accordance with your essence.

A quick and powerful stress reliever, meditation helps you to mentally back off for a few minutes, allowing your natural common sense and wisdom to be refreshed.

Meditation provides a welcome time-out from constant thinking about the past and the future. Re-living the past is an oxymoron. It's impossible to do. The past is dead and gone, set in historical concrete. Anticipating the future is equally impossible because of the incalculable outcomes and the inability to control all circumstances. Planning and goal-setting are necessary, but relentless future-thinking maximizes dreaming and minimizes doing.

Lessons from a Zen Sage

"Meditation, the main practice of Zen, gives people a chance to step back a little and see the situation we are in, personally and nationally, in a clearer light."
Zen teacher Cheri Huber

The benefits of meditation may be instantaneous, or they may take time to develop. Getting through the initial learning curve is key. The best way to become more comfortable with meditation is to expand your meditative practice gradually, starting with just a minute or two each day and not increasing meditation time until you see the benefits of doing so.

Meditation develops the mind, much the same way that working out at the gym with lighter weights leads to the ability to lift heavier weights.

Quick and Easy Meditation #1

1) Find a quiet, private place and sit comfortably, on a chair or on the floor. Breathe in deeply, allowing the belly to expand first, then the chest.

2) Breathe out slowly and completely, taking more time to exhale than to inhale. Try to flatten the belly while exhaling.

3) Repeat steps 1 and 2 for a minute or so.

Dealing with the Discomfort of Just Being

Despite the advantages, the simple act of sitting quietly for a few minutes in a meditative state can be more difficult for some than complex tasks such as solving a crossword puzzle, composing a symphony or translating a foreign language. Humans have taught themselves that relaxed contemplation is uncomfortable, unproductive, and must be replaced by activity…any activity.

At first meditation may seem uncomfortable and unusual. Developing the discipline and patience to stick with it for awhile is, in itself, a lesson in introspection.

A difficult aspect of meditation is dealing with random thoughts, worries and daydreams that seem to pop up continuously. Focusing on breathing—for example, counting breaths or timing inhalations and exhalations—helps to quiet down the *drill sergeant of the mind.*

When the mind is completely calm, surprisingly good things happen. You see more clearly:

- Who you are and what you value
- What you need and what you desire
- Your connection to everyone and everything in nature.

One of the first things you'll notice about meditation is how difficult it is to stay in-the-moment. With practice, in-the-moment awareness improves. Glimpses of such awareness are glimpses of enlightenment. Similar to enlightenment, in-the-moment awareness is a natural state of being that humans have allowed to be pushed aside by continually distracting thoughts. In other words, being out-of-the-moment is unnatural non-awareness.

The mind is always active. Without it you'd perish, but it doesn't know when to shut up. It will interject into peaceful, focused, enjoyable activity. It will take you away from the place you actually are, and from the people you are actually with. The hyperactive mind of the salesperson mind can barge into the middle of an intense, one-on-one conversation with a customer and shout, "I wonder what's on the agenda for the management meeting tomorrow?"

Meditation is merely a way of gaining back greater control of your mind. Competitive athletes tune their muscles. Competitive salespeople tune their minds.

Reward Yourself with a Brief Meditation

In the five minutes it takes to sip a cup of coffee, you can perform a meditation that can positively affect the rest of your day.

Whatever you are doing is the perfect time and place to increase your awareness. Calling a prospect, meeting with a customer, and listening to a coworker speak, are all excellent ways to simultaneously work and grow.

Working on yourself and your sales at the same time combines mindfulness with normal, everyday life experience. Some activities lend themselves better than others to mindfulness work. Try out mindfulness exercises with a few different activities. Use your life as a continuing experiment, and decide through introspection which combination of philosophy, mindset, and action works best for you.

The physical act of meditation is not holy, mystical or spiritual. The results, however, may be quite amazing. Meditation itself is simply:

- Sitting down
- Being still and quiet
- Slowing down the constant chatter of thoughts
- Allowing your true nature to emerge, if only for a brief time.

Meditation can be done in countless others ways besides the traditional still-and-quiet approach. Blending meditation with a favorite activity is also popular. The objective is to perform the activity with a calm, clear mind. Meditation may be practiced any time, and anywhere...in brief snippets, or for extended periods. If someone says they never meditate, they probably do—they just call it by a different name. Zen meditation includes in-the-moment immersion into activities such as:

- Fishing in the middle of a stream
- Going for a long drive on a winding road
- Sitting on the sofa, TV and radio off, lights dimmed, focusing on a single pleasant thought
- Complex mechanical or mathematical tasks such as carefully constructing a ship in a bottle or looking for patterns in a stream of radio telescope data
- Running a marathon.

Repetitive tasks that can be done safely lend themselves to such active meditation. Long distance runners often find themselves in a meditative state halfway through a run. Working a pottery wheel, playing a musical instrument and gardening are other ways to meditate while working. It may be easier at first, however, to focus on private, comfortably-seated traditional meditation.

The results of meditation vary. Sometimes you'll have a soul-moving insight. Sometimes you'll simply feel tired or bored. Sometimes you'll come away frustrated that the true nature you're discovering about yourself doesn't match your current lifestyle. When these things happen, accept the frustration, tiredness or boredom for what they are. Make no conclusions or pronouncements. Maintain your commitment to mindfulness. Your next meditation could be the missing piece of a puzzle...a piece that enables a valuable realization.

The Mechanics of Meditation

Optimally, meditation should be done:
- In a location that will be interruption-free and quiet
- In a clean, odorless area (incense is sometimes used to add the scent of pine or cedar to the air)
- In an area that is neither too cold nor too warm
- At the same time each day.

Lessons from a Zen Sage

"A quiet place is good. Prepare a thick sitting mat. Use a round cushion to support the backside. Just sit upright. Do not lean to the left, incline to the right, slump forward, or arch backward. Let the breath pass through the nose. Let the eyes be open."
Zen Master Dogen's (1200-1254) formal instructions for zazen.

Sitting zazen is the Zen term for traditional seated meditation. Zen meditation has historically been done sitting upright and cross-legged on a mat, often using a cushion below the rear of the buttocks to keep the spine straight. The *full lotus* cross-legged pose is the most difficult to master. Any floor-sitting may be physically painful after just a few minutes, if you aren't well versed in sitting cross-legged. The cause of pain is usually one or both of the following:
1. Joints, tendons and ligaments may lack flexibility.

2. Back muscles may be poorly developed from years of slouching while driving, sitting on the sofa, or being hunched over a computer keyboard.

The good news is that, with time and practice, the ability to sit cross-legged will improve, and the pain will decrease. Yoga and Pilates classes are excellent ways to work on strengthening abdominal, back and leg muscles. Regular stretching and light weight training are also recommended. As with any new physical regimen, ensure you're medically fit, learn from a qualified instructor, and start out slowly to avoid injury.

The easiest cross-legged position is the natural-feeling *Burmese*. The *half lotus* is a step toward the tough full lotus.

A perfectly acceptable alternative to sitting cross-legged on the floor is sitting on the edge of a padded chair. Another way is to kneel on the floor (using a pad or carpet), with a thick cushion between your buttocks and your legs.

Whichever position you choose, sit with a straight spine. Don't sway, and don't lean left or right, forward or backward. Relax your shoulders downward, but don't slump. Wear loose fitting clothing or loosen tight clothing to avoid discomfort while meditating.

Some people close their eyes, but daydreams and tiredness occur more frequently with eyes closed. Try to keep your eyes three-quarters open, gazing slightly downward. If such a lazy unfocused gaze is difficult because of visual distractions and temptations to look around, you may close your eyes, but take care not to doze.

Now breathe. Slow down your breaths. Breathe from your abdomen, feeling your belly expand and contract. Calm your mind. That's all there is to it. You're meditating.

Counting Breaths to Simplify Calmness of Mind

The best way to progress through meditation is by employing simple breathing techniques. Focus on breathing through meditation helps you transition from being overwhelmed by thoughts, to being aware and accepting of them, to being able to release them. Your focus on the depth and timing of inhalations and exhalations causes the brain to slow down the continuous flow of thoughts. When unwanted thoughts occur, acknowledge them and release them, and return your focus to the breath.

One way to occupy the restless, thinking mind while meditating is to assign it a mathematical task. Count "one" on the in-breath, "two" on the out-breath, "three" on the in-breath, and so on. When you sense a thought intruding, acknowledge it—without judging the thought as good or bad...merely a thought—and start over again at "one." With practice you may find there's no need to count breaths while meditating, but it's a great technique to fall back on when needed.

Exercise #6: Calmness through Counting

Step 1: Using a clock that indicates seconds, during a timed 30-second period, use your fingers to count how many thoughts pop into your head. (Thoughts are everything from "What a nice clock" to "I'm hungry" to "This is a silly exercise.")
Result (number of thoughts in 30 seconds): _____

Step 2: Now repeat the exercise while focusing on your breath. When the timed 30-second period starts, begin counting each time you in inhale ("1") and exhale ("2"), and so on ("3, 4, 5...") until time is up. Use your fingers to count how many thoughts pop into your head as you are counting breaths.
Result (number of thoughts in 30 seconds): _____

The second result is usually lower than the first. Focusing on counting breaths facilitates calmness by occupying the mind with a simple task. This is an easy way to learn meditation.

Another popular breathing focus technique involves closing alternate nostrils. Use a finger to press closed the left nostril and breathe only through the right for three full inhalations/ exhalations. Alternate to the other nostril for three breaths, then use both nostrils for three breaths, then repeat the cycle.

You'll develop your own style of meditation after awhile. Perform the meditations in this book quietly and in private, if possible. Don't be surprised if at first you are slightly unsettled by the experience. It's surprising to find out how noisy you are inside. The goal here is not enlightenment or mystical experience, but merely tranquility and calming of the mind...some time devoted just to you.

Steps for a Full Meditation

1) Sit comfortably, with a straight spine.
2) Close your eyes or leave them halfway open, whatever feels comfortable.
   a) Closing the eyes sometimes leads to sleepiness, so if that happens, open them slightly.
   b) If it helps, lightly focus on a non-moving object in front of you.
   c) Facing a mirror or a window to the outdoors may create too many visual distractions.
3) Breathe normally at first, and notice how you're doing.
   a) Are your breaths shallow? Deep?
   b) How many seconds long (count, "one one thousand, two one thousand . . .") is each inhalation?
   c) How many seconds long is each exhalation?
   d) Are you inhaling through your mouth or your nose? What about exhaling? (Either way is fine...just notice it.)
4) Extend the count of your inhalation by a second or two.
5) Extend the count of your exhalation even longer, by three of four seconds if possible.
6) Feel each inhalation swell your abdomen first, then your chest, not the other way around.
   a) It feels odd at first to expand the belly, and it may look odd too, but two inches above the navel is the center of

gravity for the body, and breath should emanate from there.

7) Feel each exhalation flatten down your abdomen, until there's almost no air left inside.

8) As you continue this deep breathing, pay attention to each thought that your mind creates.

    a) Was it a thought about the past? A thought about the future? Whichever, it drew you out of the moment...for a moment.

    b) Notice the thought, but don't immediately reject it. Acknowledge its arrival. Then allow it to drift away, leaving you once again calm and clear.

9) Become comfortable with the process of seeing, accepting and letting go of your thoughts.

    a) At first, thoughts will occur often.

    b) After awhile you'll see more time elapse between thoughts.

10) Pay attention to your body. Is something hurting? Feeling uncomfortable?

    a) Shift your sitting position if an area of your body is in pain.

    b) If areas of your body are not in pain but simply calling your attention to them, pay attention for as long as you have to, then return to the breathing meditation.

Notice what you feel when you're not thinking. Allow yourself to smile as you breathe. Some laugh with joy while meditating. Develop your own unique responses.

Start out spending only a few minutes meditating. Add more time slowly until you can go on for five, ten, perhaps fifteen minutes or more.

With a calm mind you are better equipped to pay attention to your own needs, and those of your customers.

Lessons from a Zen Sage

"What we're doing is taming our mind. We're trying to overcome all sorts of anxieties and agitation, all sorts of habitual thought patterns, so we are able to sit with ourselves. Life is difficult, we may have tremendous responsibilities, but the odd thing, the twisted logic, is that the way we relate to the basic flow of our life is to sit completely still. It might seem more logical to speed up, but here we are reducing everything to a very basic level."

Sakyong Mipham Rinpoche, *Shambhala Sun*, July 1994

"Enlightenment's prime virtue is generosity in all things."
-   Robert A. F. Thurman, Ph.D.

4

CONNECTING WITH CUSTOMERS

Sales 101

The *ZenWise Selling* approach assumes salesperson proficiency in basic skills, such as knowledge of:

- The selling company's business, priorities and objectives

- The selling company's products, features and benefits, plus their vulnerabilities

- The strong and weak points of competitive products

- Typical objections raised by customers, and proper salesperson responses

- Key questions to ask to advance the discussion to the next level.

It should be *Sales 101*, but many salespeople fail to gather this minimal level of information before first contacting a prospect or customer. Skipping these basics, and hoping that a Zen mind alone will build customer relationships, is like an artist trying to create a masterpiece with no paint.

You Can't Control the Customer

It's a misconception that successful salespeople are the best at controlling their customers. Successful salespeople are the best at *communicating and connecting with* their customers. Sales has little to do with control, and everything to do with:

- Establishing credentials and trust

- Compassionately understanding needs and biases

- Educating the customer

- Removing buying obstacles

- Keeping promises, and following-up with excellent service and support.

Still, many salespeople cling to the hope of customer control (or account control). To challenge the notion of control, try saying, "I am not in control of my customer. I cannot control what or when they buy." Those are scary words. Yet they're true.

Affirming to yourself that you don't know what the customer will do is disquieting yet liberating. The freedom that results from a not-knowing, not-controlling attitude enables you to sell with a higher degree of flexibility, creativity, partnership and connection.

Control is stress inducing for both the controller and the *controlee*. When customers see you aren't trying to control them, they relax. Relaxed customers are easier to deal with than defensive, wary, stressed-out customers.

Giving up control of your customers doesn't mean giving up on getting your message across. Just the opposite. Messages are better received under non-threatening conditions. When customer control is no longer the goal, you have more and better opportunities to express your opinions and beliefs to the customer, and to ask for theirs in return. A free, empathetic exchange of ideas helps both parties to understand the other.

Not-controlling also helps to neutralize common fears of customers, including:

- Fear of meeting new people

- Fear of meeting salespeople, in particular

- Fear of being talked into buying something

- Fear of missing something important in the fine print.

These aren't mortal, paralyzing fears, but they impede selling nonetheless. Recognizing and empathizing with these potential fears helps to soothe the dialogue into one that is non-threatening and productive.

An easy way to take pressure off a customer is for the salesperson to pull back early. Consider saying, "You know, there's a good chance our product may be overkill for you right now. We'll chat for awhile, and you'll come away with a good education about how this kind of product is affecting the future of your industry, but no hard feelings if it's not a perfect fit, okay?" The customer often exhales with relief. Their wariness is decreased, and the door is open for genuine communication and possible relationship building.

Exercise #7: List your strongest selling talents

- _____
- _____
- _____
- _____
- _____

Relationship Selling is a Mindset, Not a Technique

Relationship selling is the steady escalation of the salesperson's status from vendor to partner to trusted advisor. In the business-to-business arena, relationship selling has proven to work well. Business-to-consumer companies are fast catching on.

The key ingredient is an emotional bond — a trust — between buyer and seller. Face-to-face interaction is the preferred starting point, but even savvy online sales organizations, such as Amazon and Ebay, strive to capture repeat business through welcome-back messages and extensive customization capabilities for individual customers.

Words from the Wise
"Every price is too high, until the customer is emotionally involved."
  D. Forbes Ley

Selling involves communicating with four or five groups of people:

1) customers
2) peers
3) management
4) support personnel
5) subordinates (if applicable).

The first step in emotionally connecting with a customer is emotionally connecting with yourself. The depth and effectiveness of your communication with these people governs your success as a salesperson.

The way you communicate depends on the way you view yourself and others. See others as frustrations or impediments to your happiness and personal goals, and they will act accordingly. See others as connected to you, both through work and in a universal sense, and you have an unlimited opportunity to improve your career — and yourself — at the same time.

The First Hurdle: Establishing Trust

The best way to sell your product to a customer is to establish a relationship based on trust, honesty and integrity. If you take these principles to heart — as opposed to merely using them as sales tactics — you will be seen as genuine in the customer's eyes, and in your own. Seeing yourself as trustworthy and honest positively affects many aspects of your life, not just your role as salesperson.

The best customer relationship is one that is long-term. Repeat business is the sweetest business of all, because you don't have to work as hard for incremental orders, and you're consistently contributing to your customer's success. The customer knows you and your company, and trusts you and your product. You have proven your value.

It takes effort to create and maintain long-term, mutually-trusting relationships with customers. Unfortunately, many salespeople don't have the time, interest or desire needed to create long-term relationships. Transaction-based, *churn and burn* selling is one of the few areas in which such a salesperson may prosper.

Trust is a natural by-product of mindful selling. For salespeople who apply their personal values and ethics to their work, trust is a simple thing to establish. Reflecting your honesty and integrity in everyday dealings with prospects, customers, coworkers, subordinates and management eliminates duality, reduces stress, and simplifies your work.

Connecting With the Customer Through Compassion

Every emotion you have ever felt — sadness, joy, fear, hope, anger, love — has been felt by your customer. You are special, unique and worthy of extra care. So too is your customer. Seeing, then acting upon, this commonality sets the stage for compassion.

The result of practicing compassion is an elevation from *knowing* the customer, to *relating to* the customer. This relationship defines the customer as you, but simply playing another role. Active listening means hearing the customer's words as if you were speaking them yourself. Doing so limits the tendency to mentally disconnect and prepare your reply while the customer is still speaking. Without active listening skills, salespeople will have difficulty establishing customer connections.

Connecting with the customer entails a constant effort to avoid distractions and to stay in-the-moment as much as possible. When an unrelated or disruptive thought finds its way into your mind, simply acknowledge it, make a brief mental or written note if it's important, and return your attention to the customer.

The Zen mind sees itself as connected with the world, with every person, and with every thing. Connection requires compassion and empathy, two terms usually reserved for intimate relationships. But why limit the experiences of compassion and empathy to close, personal relationships? They are equally applicable and rewarding at work.

Compassion is either sympathetic or empathic. Expressing sympathy is, "I know what you're going through." Empathy is, "I feel what you're going through." A salesperson/customer connection is strong when sympathetic, but even stronger when empathetic. Think of it as relationship selling, taken to a deeper level: compassionate selling.

Compassionate selling is not magic, and it doesn't always result in success. It takes *two to tango* for any relationship to work. Customers have bad days, just as you do. Your inability to create a connection with a customer may reflect their lack of interest in you, your product, or your company. The customer may have personal reasons or issues that prevent a connection from occurring. Whatever the cause, your compassionate, empathetic selling efforts will sometimes be poorly received. When this happens, realize two things:

1. You have lost nothing by your attempt at establishing a compassionate connection.
2. Your attempt has left an initial, positive impression that may help later sales efforts.

Becoming skilled at creating compassionate customer relationships will positively affect your life outside of sales. Your job as a salesperson is a test-bed, a proving ground, for personal growth and expanded awareness. When you deliver the best *you* to your customers, self-improvement occurs effortlessly.

Exercise #8: Compassion on the Road

When driving and seeing the driver behind you following too closely and looking upset, do you:

☐ Look for a way to allow them to pass?
☐ Tap the brakes just enough to alert them?
☐ Apply the brakes hard to scare them?

From a compassionate viewpoint it's possible—regardless of how likely—that the driver was just informed that their child is in the hospital after an accident at school. Their driving is poor and potentially dangerous because of their desire to get to hospital fast, not to annoy you by tailgating. If you were in a similar predicament, you may drive the same way. Disconnecting from the offended ego (*"How dare they do that to me?"*) is the first step in compassionate thinking and increased awareness.

The Underrated Art of Listening

Customer connections are built and enhanced by good listening.

One of the toughest things for a salesperson to do while a customer is speaking is to quiet down the distracting chatter of the mind. These unwanted *mental pop-up ads* are ostensibly trying to help, yet they seldom do. A quiet mind listens much better than a distracted mind. As the customer speaks, the salesperson's mind can bark out commands and suggestions at a sometimes fantastic rate, including morsels such as:

- "Don't forget to bring up the self-configuration feature of my product."
- "If I don't close this sale I'll have to scramble to make my quota."
- "I'll really bury the competition with my next remark."
- "What the heck is she rambling on about? I have an important statement to make!"

Failure to listen well to a customer is a damaging omission. Make this mistake early on, and the relationship may wither before it grows. Make it as you're trying to close the sale, and you may not see red flags before it's too late. Often the answer to, "I have no idea why I lost that sale," is poor listening.

Customers know when you aren't really listening to them. How?

- Your eye contact falters
- You interrupt them to make your points
- You finish their sentences for them
- Your statements don't match the customer's stated needs and issues.

The first thing you gain by listening well to your customer is their respect. Being listened to feels good. Being understood feels even better. Those feelings are often reciprocated back to the salesperson, in the form of customer attention to what you're saying, and what you're selling. Call it *conversation karma*.

One way to demonstrate to your customer that you are listening is to paraphrase back to them the main points they make. "So you're saying that…" This has the added benefit of solidifying in your mind the customer's main areas of need, including their biases and views about the industry, the competition, and your company.

Sometimes Customers Lie

The closer you listen to a customer, the better you'll be able to detect lies, omissions and half-truths. Detecting such misinformation is valuable when creating a sales strategy and when deciding whether or not to pursue the customer.

When they first begin to speak, children do not lie. It is a learned phenomenon. Those suffering from autism neither lie nor comprehend lies. The autistic world is a lonely one, however. For the rest of the world, lying is sometimes considered an art form capable of being refined to great levels. Some people are congratulated on their ability to lie.

Worth a Smile

When approaching the Pearly Gates a person confesses that they have told 50,000 lies in their lifetime. Seeing the gatekeeper's apprehension the person adds, *"But they were only lies to salespeople."* The Gates immediately swing wide open and the person is warmly welcomed inside.

The average person tells three lies each day, according to psychotherapist Laurie Weiss, Ph.D. Customers will lie because:

- They believe the lie will be easier to deliver — or be more easily accepted — than will the truth.
- They don't want you to know that they really don't understand your product.
- They have something to hide regarding their relationship with the current supplier.
- They are bored with you and they want you to stop speaking.

Most do poorly when tested for the ability to detect lies in others. Although far from absolute or foolproof, here are some signs that a person is lying:

- Their body, hand and finger movements fit unnaturally with the words they're speaking.
- They pause too long before answering.
- There is less eye contact—or more blinking—than used in previous answers.
- They look downward while speaking. (Upward glances often denote truthful thought.)
- Their vocal pitch raises.
- They smile less, or they smile falsely for too long.

Keep in mind that these signs are relatively well known, especially among the community of habitual liars. Therefore the signs may be deliberately suppressed, and the listener is successfully fooled.

Knowing that lies happen enables the salesperson to plan accordingly for contingencies. Verify information given. Do your homework. Most of all, listen with your eyes, as well as your ears.

If you never misrepresent facts and always maintain your commitment to an honest relationship with your customers, you are setting the stage for mutual sincerity to occur. When a leader takes a higher path, others tend to follow.

Exercise #9: List the times a customer told you a complete lie that affected the sale

- _____
- _____
- _____
- _____
- _____

Strategic Selling

After you've met with a customer and established an initial connection, the next step is to customize your message and decide how best to deliver it. This is your sales strategy.

The goal of a sales strategy is to secure from the customer an agreement to purchase. A sales strategy is made up of short- and long-term plans to educate and guide the customer in recognizing the compelling benefits and problem-solving elements of your products as superior to those of the competition.

To create a sales strategy you must first identify and understand the customer's:

- Overall business objective or corporate mission statement
- Problems and painful areas that require solutions
- Needs — both immediate and long-term
- Biases and favorites — in companies, products and people
- Position, standing and level of influence within their organization.

Customers may be unclear about their own problems, needs and biases. Sometimes they're even unclear about their own level of influence. An important part of a sales strategy is helping the customer clearly define — and perhaps even discover — their problems. For corporate customers, some common problem areas that may need uncovering as part of a strategic selling plan include:

- Poor productivity or time management
- Poor financial performance
- Poor access to information
- Poor sales
- Poor corporate image or employee morale.

Equipped with this information, you can begin to structure a methodology for communicating your message to the customer.

Without this information, you'll be delivering a standard sales pitch and hoping that it sticks. Such a *non-strategy* may be cost- and time-effective for transaction-oriented selling such as tele-marketing sales of newspaper subscriptions and long distance services, but it won't be successful in most sales campaigns.

One strategy does not fit all. If you are actively selling to ten different customers, then you may require ten different strategies. A great strategy for one customer may be the absolute worst approach for another. A one-size-fits-all methodology leaves open the potential for surprise because of assumptions that are made. Surprise, while an everyday part of sales, is best minimized whenever possible.

Exercise #10: List what you want to change about the way you sell, prospect or present

- _____
- _____
- _____
- _____
- _____

Brainstorming as a Team Sport

Creating a customer strategy requires open-minded brain-storming that, temporarily at least, throws out pre-conceived notions about what customers typically want. If you *are* the team then brainstorming will be a solo activity. If a team of individuals is involved with a particular customer, gather them together for a strategy brainstorming session.

Meet in a quiet room and eliminate or minimize distractions and interruptions. After the team leader goes over the basics about the customer, begin a wide open, nothing-is-a-crazy-idea discussion. For time management purposes, consider an agenda such as:

- 30 minutes for brainstorming
- 10 minutes to select best ideas
- 20 minutes to draft the action plan.

Write down all ideas and observations rapidly and without prejudice or organization. Use paper, keyboard, white-board or flip-chart...whatever works. When all free-form thoughts are exhausted, begin connecting—using arrows, numbers or symbols—related ideas together. Create categories. The objective is to form a compelling, personalized sales strategy that will serve as a flowchart for selling to the customer.

Leave open the possibility that, as more information is gathered from customer conversations, the strategy may have to be modified, or perhaps even recreated.

Whether strategizing solo or as a team, when you reach a problem area or one that seems to have few solutions, don't think harder, think easier. Take a break or a time out. Tell a joke. Mentally back away from the problem and defocus for a minute. Forced thinking is repetitive thinking, illuminating the same facts and observations repeatedly. Better answers appear when the mind is less knotted.

Words from the Wise

"...When great athletes were asked what they were thinking during their best performance, they universally declared that they weren't thinking very much at all. They reported that their minds were quiet and focused."

Timothy Gallwey, author of *The Inner Game of Tennis*

When completed, keep the sales strategy in a safe place and refer to it often. When a sales proposal is made, use the strategy. When a sales presentation is created, use the strategy. When formulating a closing proposition, use the strategy.

Educating the Customer

Educating the customer in the ways your product solves their problems takes you part-way toward a successful sale. This education may not be a brief process. The salesperson may have to expend significant time and effort. If, during the information gathering and message delivery phases, it appears a sale is not likely because of poor product fit, customer bias or any other reasons, consider whether or not investing more time and effort is worthwhile. This is sometimes referred to as an *opportunity cost assessment*.

Knowledge of your customer's viewpoints is essential to the design and presentation of effective selling messages. With the customer's perceptions in mind, design your message and presentation methods accordingly. Examples of message planning topics include:

- What information about your products will you teach the customer?

- What information about your company will you teach the customer?

- What information about the industry and the competition will you teach the customer?

- What information about *you* will you teach the customer?

- What kind of relationship do you want to have with the customer?

Getting your message heard is best done in an easy-to-understand, concise format. Clearly state how each product element addresses a particular customer need. Specifics are far better than generalities, and examples of other customers — especially referencable customers in the same industry — who have successfully implemented your company's products are especially compelling.

An example of a customized, customer-centric *benefit message* is:

"Spacely Corporation's remote-to-headquarters network performance will increase tenfold to 50 megabits per second by implementing our accelerator solution. Such an increase will allow uploads to occur 10 times faster, thereby allowing nightly back-ups to finish before 2 a.m., and early-morning code upgrades to be installed before first-shift arrival at 7 a.m. The bottom line is that your staff will have an additional 300 man-hours each week to focus on revenue generation, instead of on current maintenance activities."

Once your educational message has been delivered, make sure it was understood by requesting feedback from the customer. Ask questions. What do they think? How did it go? Has there been a shift in their perceptions? A trial close at this point is perfectly acceptable. Stay attuned to buying signals. If they're ready to buy, close the sale!

Dazzle Them with Preparation and Follow-Through

In a survey, *Purchasing Magazine* asked hundreds of purchasing managers for their opinions on the most desirable qualities in salespeople.[6] The results were, in order of importance:

1. Basic thoroughness and follow-through

2. "Going the extra mile"

3. Market knowledge

4. Keeping the customer informed

5. Willingness and ability to expedite product or service delivery

6. Consistency

7. Creativity.

The same survey showed that a salesperson is seen as *ineffective* when they:

*   Have little product knowledge

*   Have little knowledge about the customer

*   Haven't prepared for meetings and presentations

*   Show up late for appointments

*   Are pushy or aggressive.

A stinging comment came from Mike Horricks of Collins & Aikman Interior Systems Inc., who said, "Most salespeople are not prepared, and they do not offer me any real solutions to problems. I need someone who can offer real cost reductions and real solutions. Most of us are so busy we barely have time to look at new items."

Don't promise more than you can deliver to the customer, but follow-up rapidly and completely on the promises you make. Even little things are important. If you mention a trade article to a customer, they express interest in seeing it, and you promise to send them a copy later on, be sure to write down the promise in your notes and send it to the customer that evening. (Evening emails to customers also indicate how hard you are working for them.)

If you fail to send the article, the customer may not remind you of it, but they will remember your forgetfulness. When managers, peers or support personnel accompany you on a sales call, pay attention to the commitments they make to the customer. If they don't deliver on their promises, it will reflect negatively on you, the primary account manager. The number of slip-ups the customer allows you before deciding that you and your company are unreliable is never known in advance. Assume a low number.

The ultimate compliment from a customer to a salesperson is when they tell other prospective buyers that you are trustworthy, knowledgeable and helpful.

Cultivating Repeat Business

Closing a deal with a customer is not the end of a transaction, but the beginning. Receiving funds for goods or services should spur an elevated level of communications between you and your customer. Failing to see this—and merely completing the initial transaction and walking away—is the epitome of leaving money on the table...a high crime in the world of sales.

Ensure that good sales don't turn bad. A *Harvard Business Review* article highlights the need for a social contract between salesperson and customer. The article states, "Because the parties have failed to have a true meeting of the minds, they sign a deal that is likely to fall apart. To avoid such a disastrous outcome...discuss the details of [the] social contract before inking the deal. For instance, what is the real nature, extent, and duration of the agreement? And in practice, how will we make decisions, handle unforeseen events, communicate with one another, and resolve disputes?"[7]

Create a customized *checklist of post-sale actions* for your product or service. Use your checklist to help prevent misunderstandings, and to create a safe, trusting, long-lasting relationship, between you and the customer. Here's an example of a checklist that is suitable when selling a high-end product to a customer.

1. Gather from the customer complete contact information for all personnel who will be involved in the implementation of your product.

2. Provide the customer with complete contact information for all of your personnel who will be involved in delivering, installing and supporting your product.

3. Provide the customer with an escalation procedure to follow if they have questions and problems with your product.

4. Provide the customer with average and maximum response times for return communications once they report a problem.

5. Provide the customer with an emergency method of communicating with you if the escalation procedure fails.

6. Speak with the customer to ensure that they understand the duration (start and end dates) and terms and conditions of post-sale service and support.

7. Speak with the customer to ensure that they understand the cost of renewing post-sale service and support once the initial period expires.

8. Agree to a schedule of follow-up conversations with the customer, to gauge their level of satisfaction.

An Affirmation Meditation for Salespeople

With one deal closed, it's time to jump right in and close the next one, right? Actually, it depends on whether or not you're physically, mentally and emotionally running in an optimal mode. If so, then go on to the next opportunity. If not, try this affirmation meditation designed to re-center and re-energize salespeople.

This simple affirmation meditation will improve your mental acuity and emotional calmness. Do not use this meditation to contemplate specific sales and work-related problems. It's more general than that. Read through the steps before you begin the meditation. Then find a quiet, private place and begin breathing slowly and deeply. As you inhale, tell yourself the following words, using softly spoken words or non-verbal thoughts. As you exhale, clear your mind and extend the exhalation longer than the inhalation.

- ⊛ Inhale with, "I am a good person." Exhale slowly.
- ⊛ Inhale with, "I am a good salesperson." Exhale slowly.
- ⊛ Inhale with, "I choose happiness." Exhale slowly.
- ⊛ Inhale with, "I will help others find happiness." Exhale slowly.
- ⊛ Inhale with, "When I feel sad I won't escape." Exhale slowly.
- ⊛ Inhale with, "When I feel sad I will look inside." Exhale slowly.
- ⊛ Inhale with, "I will know my fears." Exhale slowly.
- ⊛ Inhale with, "I will let fear go when I am ready." Exhale slowly.
- ⊛ Inhale with, "The past is gone." Exhale slowly.
- ⊛ Inhale with, "The future is unknown." Exhale slowly.
- ⊛ Inhale with, "I have this moment." Exhale slowly.
- ⊛ Inhale with, "I will calm my mind." Exhale slowly.
- ⊛ Inhale with, "I will simply breathe." Exhale slowly.
- ⊛ Inhale with, "I will simply be." Exhale slowly.
- ⊛ Repeat once or twice more.

"Chance favors the prepared mind."
- Louis Pasteur

5

THE ZEN OF PROSPECTING

Connected in Fifteen Seconds

When you call a prospect on the telephone they will form an opinion about you within fifteen seconds of hearing your voice. The words you choose, and the way you say them, will greatly affect whether you schedule a meeting with the customer, or hearing them say, "Thanks for the call, but I'm not interested."

Prospects you first meet face to face form opinions even faster. Non-verbal cues say more than your choice of words. The way in which you initially engage the prospect, establish eye contact, smile, and shake their hand, will all be tabulated to form an instant impression—correct or not—about you and the company you represent.

Conversations with the prospect's gatekeeper (receptionist, assistant or secretary) are instrumental at establishing rapport and respect. Prospects rely on their gatekeepers, and failure to impress at the pre-prospect level will directly affect your ability to secure a telephone or in-person audience with the prospect.

When you approach a prospect for the first time: 1) have a reason to call, 2) truly believe in the product you are selling, 3) respect your prospect's time, and 4) establish credibility and trustworthiness as soon as possible. Examined in detail:

1) **Have a reason to call.**

    Laws protecting consumers from unwanted telephone solicitation (including the U.S. government FTC/TSR "Do not call" registry) underscore the need for sales professionals to consider not just *who* they're calling, but *why*.

Answering a ringing telephone is often interruptive, but if the product or service offered is based on the prospect's known interests—as opposed to the prospect's listing in a telephone directory—then there is a valid reason to call.

2) **Truly believe in the product you are selling.**

This can be difficult unless you are selling—within your vertical market and geography—the best product or the best value.

Before a prospect accepts such a claim, you must see the claim as true. Your genuine, enthusiastic belief in the superiority of your company's product is a required first step in prospecting. If you don't believe, why should your prospect? Furthermore, if you don't believe it, your prospect will likely sense it, and credibility is lost.

3) **Respect your prospect's time.**

Before launching into a pitch, ask if it's okay to take sixty seconds of their time to ask them a few questions. Perhaps you are calling at a bad time, maybe they are in a meeting, or completing a report for their manager. If they agree and your conversation lasts more than a minute, the prospect is indicating interest and may be on the way to becoming a customer.

If you aren't calling at a good time, ask if a certain day and time (for example, Friday at 3 p.m.) is okay for a brief callback. Propose a second day and time if the first isn't good. Take the burden off the prospect. They didn't ask for your initial phone call, so make the call-back as easy as possible for them.

If you already have the prospect's email address, consider sending a tie-down email, such as, "Sorry we weren't able to connect today. I look forward to speaking with you Friday at 3 p.m."

Be prompt on your call-back, and again ask permission for a minute of their time. Remember, you haven't yet earned the right to expect anything from the prospect.

4) **Establish credibility and trustworthiness as soon as possible.**

Credibility and trustworthiness take time to demonstrate, but you don't have much time to do this when initially speaking with a prospect. The primary building blocks of credibility are knowledge, experience and enthusiasm. Before calling prospects, practice and perfect your personal *statement of credibility*. Neatly wrap up your why-I'm-a-helpful-expert-in-your-industry statement into a short, informative, perhaps slightly humorous story. But remember, you only have fifteen seconds.

The best way to establish credibility with a new prospect is to mention that someone in their industry whom they know suggested that you call. Be sure that the reference is valid and will vouch for you if the prospect checks. Another credibility builder, short of a personal referral, is to reference similar companies for whom your company has solved problems.

Trustworthiness, to a prospect, means they feel safe in disclosing personal and company information to you. Prospects must feel that you won't exploit their disclosures.

One way to establish trust is to be the first one to disclose...the first one to share something personal. Self-
disclosure sets the stage for communicative intimacy, yet
all prospects react differently. Don't be surprised or offended if the prospect fails to respond to your disclosures.

Credibility and trust-building through self-disclosure is
more interesting when wrapped in a story. Reveal interesting elements about yourself, your company, and the industry. Avoid slamming the competition, disguised as
disclosure, as in, "Did you hear that MediPlastic's stock
fell this morning?" Such a thin veil highlights your slant
toward ulterior motives, and destroys—instead of builds—
credibility.

The outcome of credibility and trust-building is the prospect's confidence in your ability to help solve their problems or address their needs, and in your commitment to
keep private the information they share with you.

Telephone Prospecting

On the phone, the prospect "sees" you as you see yourself. If
you see yourself as arrogant and pushy that's how you'll come
across. Stressed out and worried? That's how you'll be perceived.
If you smile to yourself while placing the phone call, however, the
customer will hear your smile, and they may respond as most
people do when receiving a smile: they return the favor.

Before picking up the telephone to dial a prospect, say the following affirming statement to yourself (saying it out loud works
best):

**"I am calm and confident, and I have something of value to
offer."**

This affirmation sets the tone for telephone prospecting calls to follow. It reduces the jitters because, even if the prospect is not interested, you have offered something of value, and nothing—neither your dignity nor your self-esteem—has been taken away from you. Equally important is the confidence the affirmation instills. The prospect hears a voice that is not calling out of desperation, but out of an informative offer for a valuable product.

When stating your name, title, company, and the purpose of your call, be sure to speak clearly. The surest way to start off on the wrong foot is to compel the prospect to say, "I'm sorry, who is this? I couldn't understand you."

The telephone is a great tool to create immediate, person-to-person contact with prospects, yet telephone prospecting also has its problems. When making outbound calls, the salesperson is susceptible to interruption from the telephone itself. When an incoming call is answered, the mind must change focus, and momentum may be lost. Consider placing outbound prospecting calls from a phone that doesn't ring.

Scheduling outbound prospecting calling times—and sticking to your schedule—keeps prospecting focused and uninterrupted. Similarly, scheduling time in which incoming phone calls are answered by your voice mail, and not you, eliminates interruptions so you can focus on prospect research, account strategy planning, brainstorming, or renewing, relaxing quiet time.

The old adage about calling executive-level customers on the phone before and after regular working hours, to avoid gatekeepers, has withstood the test of time. Telephone prospecting done early and late can yield great results. Avoid prospecting on personal numbers, however. Just because you can reach a prospect during a particular moment—a weekend, or late at night, for example—doesn't mean you should.

One of the oddest situations when making prospecting phone calls is an unwanted, protracted conversation with someone who isn't interested in your product, but who loves to chit-chat nonetheless. Instead of abruptly terminating such a call for being nonproductive, see their talkative style as a perfect opportunity to ask for help. Listen politely, then ask the prospect for suggestions of names and numbers of others they know who may be interested in your product. Using the word "help" in your request—as in, "I wonder if you can help me?"—will resonate with a chatty, friendly prospect who is likely bored at work.

Do You Know Enough to Call?

Center yourself before making a single phone call to a prospect. Take the time to breathe deeply and remember why you're selling, what you value, and what you want. If you want credibility, be knowledgeable. Know the industry, know the prospect's company, know the competition, know your company's value proposition, know how to handle objections, and know what you want from each phone call.

Above all, be respectful of the prospect. The way you treat your customers is a reflection of how you treat yourself, and vice versa.

Without doing up-front homework about how your product will fit into the prospect's business, and without respect for the prospect's time, telephone prospecting may end up as this example of a harried computer systems executive answering the phone and hearing an unfamiliar voice say:

☞ *"Mr. Blire?"*
    ☜ "It's actually Blaire. Who is this, please?"
☞ "Mr. Brail, this is Frank Schmooze with FinkNet. I'd like to talk to you about our fantastic new FinkServer."
    ☜ "I'm happy with my current server company, but thanks for calling…"
☞ *"Are you happy with being overcharged?"*
    ☜ "I've done my research and I'm satisfied. Now if you don't mind I'm right in the middle of…"
☞ *"So you're willing to pay thousands more than you have to?"*
    ☜ "Listen, I wish you luck, but I really have to…"

☞ *"If you'll just listen to me…"*

CLICK! The phone call is over, and the unprepared, pushy salesperson has forever lost the right and the ability to call that executive. The reasons should be obvious:

- The entire conversation was adversarial.
- The salesperson knew nothing about the company.
- The salesperson demonstrated no compassion for the prospect's individual problems.
- The entire conversation was the product of an anxious, fearful salesperson who saw an opportunity to complete a transaction, and not an opportunity to create a new relationship.

Now, here's the same phone call initiated by a sales rep who has done some up front homework, and who treats the prospect with respect:

☞ *"Mr. Blaire?"*
    ☜ "Yes. Who is this?"
☞ *"Mr. Blaire, this is Frank Schmooze with FinkNet. I wonder if I could have sixty seconds of your time to ask you about a story I read in a trade magazine last week? Apparently your company is expanding into the San Diego area?"*
    ☜ "That's right. But not until August. What can I do for you?"
☞ *"Well, I also discovered that your company uses Seaside as your standard server, and that you perform huge nightly data backups. FinkNet is offering a no-charge training session for current Seaside customers. In one-hour you'll learn how to cut nightly backup times in half. We'll also show you how to equip your new San Diego office for about half the cost of a Seaside implementation."*
    ☜ "Interesting, but now is a bad time to talk. I'm right in the middle of a meeting."

☞ *"I completely understand. I can call back at a better time, to give you a few more details, so you can decide if you'd like to reserve a spot for the training. Is 10 a.m. tomorrow okay for me to call again?"*
　　🖝 *"Make it 11."*
☞ *"Excellent. I'll speak with you then. Have a great day."*

There was certainly more preparation time required for the second conversation example, but the odds of a positive outcome are correspondingly higher. Decide which you will focus on: *quality prospecting* or *quantity prospecting*.

Handling "No"

Dealing with rejection is one of the toughest aspects of telephone prospecting. The dislike or fear of hearing "no" after "no" keeps many away from a career in sales. "No" is not sales failure, however. It's simply a necessary step closer to the elusive "yes."

Words from the Wise
"I am not judged by the number of times I fail, but by the number of times I succeed [which] is in direct proportion to the number of times I can fail and keep on trying."
　Tom Hopkins, *How to Master the Art of Selling*[8]

The salesperson must emotionally recover from the disappointment of the previous rejection before making the next prospecting call. Emotional recovery can take mere seconds, or much longer. Reestablishing your smiling, upbeat selling attitude can't occur until you first accept the last prospect's "no." Saying to yourself, "Okay, they weren't interested," taking a deep breath, and repeating the affirmation, *"I am calm and confident, and I have something of value to offer,"* will help you to re-center and move on to the next call with a positive attitude.

Refining Your Message

Consider refining your prospecting message and style if your success-to-call ratio is low. The key is taking away the prospect's wariness of being sold to. A poor selling message is, "Will you please buy my product?" "No," is the quickest and simplest way for a customer to reply to that message, to escape from the interrupting phone call, and to return to their work. Sometimes salespeople are allowed to ramble on for awhile because the sympathetic prospect hates to disappoint anyone. The salesperson's desperate words are merely tuned out until the prospect finds a way to gently let them down. "Listen, you sound like a nice person, but..."

Find a way to prospect using non-threatening conversation, through a two-way exchange of ideas, observations and viewpoints. Intuition and the Zen beginner's mind are both important here. Ask questions. Listen more than you talk. You can't read a prospect's mind, but you can be sensitive and agile enough to guide the discussion based on the prospect's words. Don't be afraid to gracefully end the discussion yourself when it appears that product interest is unlikely.

Exercise #10: List how you prepare for a prospecting call

- _____
- _____
- _____
- _____
- _____

Advancing the Discussion

If and when the prospect signals interest in, or agreement with, your selling message, be prepared to expertly advance the discussion to the next level.

Some calls go extremely well right from the start. The best result of a prospecting call is immediate buying interest from the customer. If that happens, use a *trial close* such as, "If I can deliver that product on Monday, at the price we discussed, are you willing to place your order today?"

Whether attempting to close a sale on the first call or to merely advance the process, always be prepared to handle an in-depth discussion of your products by knowing pricing, financing, configurations and options available, competitive positioning and a sample return on investment analysis.

If appropriate, have your calendar ready and schedule a meeting with the prospect. Ask them what they'd like to see in a face-to-face meeting. Ask them what they'd prefer *not* to see. Ask them how much time you will have. Ask for information on others who may be attending. Gather their full contact information and send them an email or note saying, "I enjoyed our conversation," and include a meeting reminder. Above all, thank them for their time and promise them an informative, useful meeting. Then deliver on your promise.

In-Person Prospecting

When prospecting face to face, approach and engage the person with visible respect. Make good eye contact and smile, but don't assume a familiarity that doesn't yet exist.

Consider something that sets you apart from other salespeople. A slight bow, when performed simultaneously with the standard handshake conveys a sense of reverence to your prospect that they won't quickly forget. This almost imperceptible tilt of the upper body demonstrates respect before the first words of dialog are exchanged.

Following the path of respect, when meeting with a prospect in their office, never answer your ringing cell phone or press buttons on your pager. It's best to have such devices turned off, or at least on quiet-buzz mode. If the prospect is in your office, the same advice applies, even if they choose to answer their cell phone in the middle of the meeting. The prospect's behavior doesn't dictate yours.

Salespeople with families and loved ones need to be reachable in emergencies, even if the salesperson is in a meeting. The best way to ensure that emergency calls from home get through is to:

- Ask loved ones to call during working hours only when urgency dictates.
- Ask loved ones to call from a phone that does not hide their caller ID. (Permanent called ID hiding can be overridden on a per-call basis.)
- Casually glance at the incoming caller ID and only answer if it appears to be an emergency.
- Be honest with the prospect: "I apologize. This is my twelve year-old daughter and she's home alone. I need to briefly take this call." Most people will understand.

Prospecting Via Email, Letters and Fax

Similar to scheduling dedicated telephone prospecting time, schedule specific times in front of your computer to write prospecting emails, and to write and send prospecting letters. During these times, resist the urge to answer the phone or read incoming email. When such interruptions require you to divert attention away from what you were doing, you may lose the ability to complete your prospecting session.

Reading and replying to emails as soon as they come in is as unproductive as having a sign on your office door that says, "Please come in and interrupt me, no matter what I'm doing, or with whom I'm meeting."

Email is a terrific way to convey well-thought-out messages to prospects and existing customers. Using the familiar copy-and-paste function, you can deliver a similar yet customized message to many prospects, thereby streamlining outgoing communications.

Something to Consider

In 2004 the U.S. federal government enacted CAN-SPAM, a law that requires unsolicited commercial e-mail messages be contain non-deceptive subject lines and clear opt-out instructions. Violations carry stiff penalties. An FTC "do-not-email" registry—similar to the FTC's "do-not-call" registry—may be next. For the mindful salesperson such legislation should have little effect. Sending mass junk emails is no way to sell products or services. Research-driven marketing and respectful, value-added prospecting remains the most effective method of reaching out to new customers.

Excellent writing style and skill conveys a positive message to a prospective customer. Unfortunately the reverse is also true. Poor writing almost always carries a negative connotation to the reader. Make sure your written communications—even brief, casual notes—are properly punctuated and free from spelling errors. Inattention to detail and affinity for shortcuts are personal traits that are conveyed by the way you write.

Conciseness and clarity are key in writing. Deliver the point quickly and completely. Prospecting emails should be no more than a paragraph or two, with a web link if applicable. When asking for a reply, do so clearly, to help the reader know what is expected, and when.

After a positive phone conversation with a prospect, follow up with a call-to-action email. In this crucial beginning of a relationship—in which a prospect could become a customer—project yourself professionally and courteously. Keep the follow-up email brief. It's clear to see which of these two follow-up emails gets the point across while eliminating superfluous words:

1) "Mr. Burg, I just wanted to say thank you for the very good conversation you and I had on the phone today around noon. Our regional vice president, Bill Stockyer, will be in town next Monday, and he has expressed interest in meeting with you, to better explain our company's customer service philosophy. If you have time around 2

p.m. next Monday, please reply to me so that I can arrange the meeting. Best regards, Sharon."

2) "Mr. Burg, Thank you for your time on the phone today. Our regional VP would like to discuss our customer service philosophy with you in person. Is Monday at 2 p.m. okay? Best regards, Sharon."

Type emails to customers off-line, and not live in the email text screen. If you've ever accidentally hit *Send* before completing your email, you know what confusion can follow. Emails titled "Please ignore my previous incomplete email" will almost assuredly have the curious reader carefully scrutinizing your previous incomplete email for the embarrassing gaffe. There's nothing quite like a salesperson's blunder to put a smirk on a customer's face.

Etiquette in writing is often overlooked. On email *To:* lines, for example, address all involved members of the prospect's staff. Placing a manager's subordinates in the *Cc:* line may be viewed as a lack of respect for such people, and may negatively affect budding relationships.

Consider the tone of your written words to prospects. Does it match the prospect and their industry? Does it match your personal speaking style? It's better if your spoken and written styles match, unless your spoken style is of so casual a nature that the reader can become confused or insulted when seeing it on paper, as in: "*Yo, Frankie! Ya gotta be nuts not to check out this stuff!*"

Clearly state your objective and call-to-action in emails and letters sent to prospects. Do the same in advertisements directed toward specific groups of prospects. Most don't like to think of themselves as capable of being persuaded to act, but a well-written communication can compel action based on need. If the product benefit is truly convincing, then the prospect may not mind the persuasion.

Accuracy is important in written communications. Check your facts and figures. Your communication may fall into the hands of your competitor. Hope that it won't, but assume that it will.

Untrue or misleading statements, especially about a competitor's company or products, may come back to haunt you. Even more damaging is the credibility you'll lose—or never achieve—if a prospect uncovers untruths.

When using email to reach prospects for the first time, your message may be seen as spam. To avoid this, inform the prospect why they are being emailed by you, and how you got their contact information. Provide simple ways for the recipient to reach you for more information, or to request that no more emails be sent.

Emails to prospects will be opened, read and acted upon more often if follow these guidelines:

- Don't send attachments.
- Virus-check all outgoing mail.
- Use an *attention-getting – but not misleading – subject* to the email or letter, designed to catch their interest and per- suade them to read on.
- Use a *strong opening sentence* that accurately conveys your central message.
- Use a clear *call-to-action* that defines the prospect's reward for completing the action.
- Avoid the use of hyperbole, such as "Free" this, or "No Charge" that.
- Avoid ALL CAPS and the misuse of exclamation points!!!
- End with a professional email signature that contains your name, title and full contact information. Avoid personal, political or religious blurbs ("Go Redskins!").
- Write a memorable or funny postscript ("p.s. ___") after your signature to encourage response.

Something to Consider

Do *not* send unsolicited faxes to prospects. It uses their fax machine time, paper and ink. In addition to being expensive, *junk faxes* are simply annoying. They are also illegal in many areas.

Meditation at Work

A long session of prospecting can become counterproductive if breaks aren't taken. When you take a break, make it a useful one. Stand up, walk around and get some fresh air before hitting the phones (or the showroom) again. Consider a brief at-work meditation.

Meditation at home—before or after work, and during weekends—is preferred over meditation at work, to avoid interruptions from email, telephone and coworkers. At-work meditation has its benefits however, and it's possible to squeeze one in during the briefest of free time periods, or whenever you feel the desire to calm your brain and enjoy a few moments of peaceful clarity.

When you feel yourself becoming stressed or exhausted at work, a brief in-the-office meditation can help. If you're nervous before a forecast review meeting with your manager, or if you've just ended such a meeting and you're feeling irritable, try meditating for a few minutes.

Quick and Easy Meditation #2

Find a quiet, private place and sit comfortably, either on a chair or on the floor. Say the following words softly to yourself as you breathe slowly, with belly expanding on the inhalation, and taking longer than usual to exhale:

1) "Breathing in, I calm body and mind"
2) "Breathing out, I smile"
3) "Breathing in, I notice this moment"
4) "Breathing out, I enjoy this moment"

Repeat steps 1 through 4 for a minute or so.

Meditating at work may feel uncomfortable, unless your privacy is guaranteed, or you're so self-assured that you wouldn't be bothered at all by a coworker seeing you meditate. The optimal location is private, quiet and comfortable. For those who don't have a private office, here are some creative meditation spots at work:

- In your desk chair, if you can insulate yourself from ringing phones and others speaking with you.
- In a vacant, unscheduled conference room.
- In a park or courtyard during lunch.
- In your car in the parking lot, in the roomiest seat.
- In a bathroom stall. (Multitasking okay.)

<u>6</u>
THE ZEN OF PRESENTING

Presenting...You!

The best time to build credibility, trust and confidence is when eyes meet, hands shake and ideas are exchanged in both directions. Sales presentations are the *launch pad* for customer relationships. Connections made during prospecting are grown and strengthened. As with all potential for success, potential for failure exists also. The best way to kill a relationship before it has a chance to grow is to present poorly.

The most favorable outcome of a sales presentation is an agreement to purchase. The second best outcome is an agreement on need/product compatibility and a plan for follow-up tasks that will lead to the sale. A minimally acceptable presentation outcome is an agreement to meet again.

Customers are increasingly wary of the word "presentation." They envision a slick info-mercial or a talking head droning over a dull Microsoft PowerPoint presentation. Fight this perception by describing and designing your presentation as an *overview*, a *discussion* or an *interactive roundtable*. Promising and delivering a presentation that offers the customer a custom-designed solution (and not a boilerplate) shows true initiative.

A sales presentation is not simply an oral or written display of words. Words are inert, emotionless symbols, with no guarantee of understanding by the listener or the reader. After selecting the best words to present, the manner in which they are presented becomes paramount. Educational content, presented well, offers the best chance of having your sales message correctly heard and positively acted upon.

Presentations must be two-way affairs. Both parties want their positions heard. Being clearly and completely understood by another human is a heart-warming feeling. "My voice has been heard!" From such mutual satisfaction, a rewarding relationship can develop.

Preparation Beats Winging It

Prepare for a presentation by considering what you want to happen afterward. If you have no concrete goals, success is left to chance. Generic presentations lead to generic sales results. Presentation preparation, or lack thereof, will be made apparent to the customer. Before presenting, consider:

- What is your overall strategy for this unique customer?

- What is your presentation strategy for this unique customer?

- Does your presentation match the customer's needs, position and background?

- Is your strategy-matching presentation made up of current, reliable, referencable and—most important—relevant content?

- Is your presentation visually compelling without being visually distracting?

- If all of your technology and visual aids fail during a presentation, could you carry on flawlessly without them?

- Does your presentation fit in the time allowed?

Unless they are either completely uninterested, or are ready to buy on the spot, customers will have questions during and following your presentation. Are you prepared for the questions by knowing the right answers in advance? Do you know the common objections customers will have? Do you know how to use *clarifying questions* to turn objections into opportunities, and to further demonstrate why your product is best for the customer?

If you answered "no" to one of more of these questions, correct the omission and practice your presentation in front of a coworker or manager before going in front of the customer.

Something to Consider

In ancient Greece, Socrates used skillfully constructed questions to clarify the positions of those debating him. Socrates lost few debates. This technique of clarifying questions is called the *Socratic Method*, and is widely taught in law schools today.

Be ready at any point during the formal presentation to stop and revert to a purely interactive discussion, if that's what the customer wants to do. Such an on-the-fly change from formal to free-form shows the customer your flexibility and your commitment to making a deeper connection. Encourage the customer to speak. In the context of a sales presentation, what the customer has to say is more important than what you have to say.

When planning a presentation, start with a standard presentation template such as the one below, and customize it so that the customer's needs and interests are addressed:

Introduction
    a) Greetings and thanks for customer's time
    b) Introductions
    c) Subject of meeting.

Overview
a) Statement of your understanding of the customer's needs and interests. Be open to on-the-fly validation and adjustment.
b) Encouragement for the customer to state their expectations for the presentation.
c) Broad description of your product's complementary solution to the customer's needs and interests, plus bold statement about your product. Object is to have customer's eyes widen and say, "Wow!"
d) Concise description of the product's benefits to the customer. Also known as answering the customer's "What's in it for me?" question in advance.

Details
a) Main Point 1
b) Main Point 2
c) Main Point 3. Three main points — each of which contains customer-related examples and references — is the maximum.

Summary
a) Strong summation that reiterates your product's complementary solution to the customer's needs and interests.
b) Questions and answers
c) Your call for the customer's action: Purchasing details, pricing quotations, comparisons, references, follow-up meetings.
d) End the presentation on an up note.

Timing is Everything

The three saddest things to see happen to a salesperson during a presentation are:

1) Trying to squeeze and rush a presentation into a too-short time slot

2) Running out of presentation time because of too much time spent on initial topics
3) Seeing a key customer leave the presentation before the call-to-action is made.

Up front, ask for more presentation time than you need, to reduce time pressures and to allow for a post-presentation discussion. If a customer agrees to hear a presentation but allocates insufficient time, try to explain the depth of the topic and negotiate for a longer time period. Without enough time, you may be wasting the entire presentation. If they insist on the shorter period, try condensing your message before calling the whole thing off.

Something to Consider

Avoid making your main presentation during a lunch or dinner with the customer. Your message will be lost somewhere between the salad and dessert. Meals are great for relationship building, team introductions, executive involvement or as a "thank you" for an order, but not so great for presentations.

Between 10 a.m. and 3 p.m. are the best times to meet customers. Before and after, and they may be too distracted by early morning or late afternoon business issues. Monday mornings and Friday afternoons are poor times for presentations. Just before lunch is fine, especially if the customer is also open to a post-presentation restaurant meal with you. Such casual chats strengthen budding relationships. Presenting right after lunchtime isn't as dreadful as some think...just keep it relatively lively to avoid placing the customer in a postprandial drowsy state.

Before the presentation begins, go over the time constraints so everyone present knows when the meeting will end. This helps solidify the customer's attendance until the end, with your inferred statement, "I am spending my valuable time with you, Mr. Customer, so please reciprocate by spending your valuable time with me."

The Flow of the Presentation

Customers who insist on answering pages and cellular phones during your presentation are either too busy to give you their full attention, or they really aren't interested in hearing what you have to say. Some customers will do this to demonstrate their level of importance or power to you, especially during early-relationship presentations. Regardless of the causes, presentations with constant interruptions are unproductive. If the interruptions persist, ask the customer for a better day and time to return and present again.

Try to schedule customer presentations in your office or facility. You have far greater control over interruptions, and the ability to customize the presentation room into a customer-focused, customer-friendly environment.

If presenting as a team, the salesperson is responsible for reminding each presenter to turn off cell phones and pagers. If one of your coworkers leaves the presentation to answer a call or page, that coworker has sent a clear, negative signal to the customer that the call is of higher priority than the customer.

Stand when making a presentation. It focuses attention on you, and gives you the ability to direct the customer's attention to others in the room, or to graphic aids such as projections and flip charts. When operating a laptop for a PowerPoint presentation, consider using a wireless mouse. Telling a colleague to reach over and click to the next slide is distracting.

As tools such as PowerPoint have improved, the number of available gimmicks—video builds, animations, music—has increased. Avoid presentation gimmicks unless they are well thought out. If appropriate, use them to add an occasional, tasteful laugh to an otherwise long, staid presentation.

Your Unique Presenting Style

The way in which you present is extremely important. How do you appear? How do you move? How does your voice sound? Is there an energy to your presentation, or a lethargy? Are you calm and confident, or stressed out and nervous? Are you comfortable with pauses—white space—in the presentation that enable new ideas to sink in?

Nervousness is common, but the customer doesn't have to see it. If you manage your breathing, movements, eye contact and minimize verbal let-me-think fillers such as "um" and "uh," the customer won't focus on your jitters.

Something to Consider

"You can have brilliant ideas, but if you can't get the ideas across, they won't get you anywhere. The ability to communicate is everything."
Lee Iacocca[9]

Know your strengths and weaknesses. Making the most of your individual strengths, and mitigating your weaknesses, are key in preparation for presentations. Even the best, most dynamic speakers have weaknesses...they're just well-hidden. Deal with your weaknesses appropriately. Resist the urge to ignore them and hope the customer will understand, sympathize, or see them as charmingly quirky. Assume they won't.

Strengths are often combined with weaknesses. Your combination is unique. Assess your presentation abilities and adjust accordingly:

✓ Are you a gifted presenter with weak technical skills?
   o Bring along a technical co-presenter to whom you can defer tough questions.

✓ Are you nervous when speaking to groups of people?
  o Practice repeatedly—with coworkers, in the mirror, or on videotape—your spoken presentation.
✓ Are you an engineer with a dislike for salespeople and customer presentations?
  o Confess your technical slant and your lack of sales savvy in advance, but be careful not to disassociate yourself from your company's professional salespeople. Engineers who garner chuckles from customers by using anti-sales rhetoric may end up injuring the relationship between the sales rep and the customer.

Something to Consider

Winston Churchill was a chronic stutterer and he suffered from a pronounced lisp. Yet he is known as one of the greatest speakers in British Parliament. He spent hours practicing before every oration, minimizing his speech impediments, while also eliminating words and phrases that would have otherwise accentuated his problems.

A key message of Zen is to know yourself well before attempting to know others. What type of salesperson are you? Some salespeople equate presentations with show business and, if given a choice, would prefer to look great in front of the customer and deliver a mediocre message, than to look mediocre and deliver a great message. Remember that the goal of the presentation is to communicate interactively, to build relationships and to sell products. Practice excellent presentation skills and make them second nature. By doing so, the emphasis remains on the solution you're proposing, even though all eyes will be on you.

> ## Exercise #12: List what makes you creative and unique while presenting to a customer
>
> - _____
> - _____
> - _____
> - _____
> - _____

Capture Yourself on Video

Videotaping yourself is a great way to see how you truly look and sound. Don't be surprised if you are uncomfortable seeing the playback. "I don't look like that!" and "I don't sound like that!" are common exclamations. As tough as it may be to see yourself on tape, remember that on-camera professionals such as actors, musicians and television journalists constantly update and improve their speaking and non-verbal skills. Your sales career often places you in the role of presenter, so sharpen your skills accordingly.

Pay attention to the following attributes of your videotaped presentation:

- Voice
- Posture
- Movement and gestures
- Facial expressions
- Eye contact
- Overall appearance or effect.

According to researcher Albert Mehrabian, Ph.D., over half of what salespeople present to a customer is transmitted visually. Another third is how you speak, and only 7% is transmitted by the actual words spoken.[10] The fascinating yet unfortunate conclusion is that how you look and how you speak are actually more important than what you say.

Presentations Are Persuasive Storytelling

The ancient Greeks studied persuasion, and their lessons are timeless. Socrates taught that persuasion is accomplished through appeals to the logic and emotions of the listener. The right combination of logic and emotion builds a trusting bond between you and the customer. Be bold when appropriate. Use humor when appropriate. Above all, create a lasting, positive impression.

People enjoy stories. Selling is serious business, yet presentations are understood better when they are wrapped into a story. As you speak, demonstrate your knowledge of the customer and their needs, but also throw in your personal experiences and insights into what otherwise may be just another we-have-the-best-widget presentation. Remember that people buy from people, not from companies. Use your Zen mind to see the sameness that connects you to your customer.

While presenting and telling your story, use plenty of sincere eye contact, but don't use it to control...only to connect. Use your arms and hands to gesticulate. In other words, keep moving.

You'll be lucky, even with the best presentation, to capture a majority of your customer's attention. A study conducted by Shipley Associates discovered the following:

- 40% of the time: customer is reminiscing
- 20% of the time: customer is thinking ahead
- 20% of the time: customer is pursuing erotic thoughts
- 20% of the time: customer is actually listening to you![11]

The same study also found that customers listen more closely to presenters with louder, faster and higher-pitched voices than they do to those who speak softer, slower and lower. When customers are paying attention, they do so only in bursts of 5 to 8 seconds. Adults have an estimated maximum attention span of 30 seconds. The lesson here is that gaining a customer's attention is important, but so is the need to constantly re-gain their attention.

Repeat your key points several times when speaking with a customer. You'll have a better chance of making sure the key points are truly heard. Keep your main points to a maximum of three. If your company has seven reasons how customers benefit from your product, find a way to boil them down to three, or risk losing the core of your message.

The Team Presentation

Consider adding as presenters other members of the sales team involved with the customer, such as technical support specialists, inside sales reps, training specialists and sales management. You may be the primary account representative, but it's advantageous to show the customer that they are buying from a closely-knit company with teams of qualified resources, all ready to help at any time.

Don't add team members without a good reason. Having people show up to customer meetings just to fill the room or to look impressive seldom works. Customers will notice that a particular individual isn't contributing to the discussion, and will wonder why your company wastes human resources in such a way. Having more presenters than customers in a room is inappropriate, and should be avoided.

Sales teaming during presentations increases the potential for things going wrong. Show the customer a solidified team with a clear message and you'll be more impressive more than a solo salesperson with no backup. Show the customer a disorganized, unqualified or confused team and you'll have a serious strike against you.

Good communication between team members is a requirement for sports teams and sales teams alike. Everyone must know what's expected of them. Before a team meets with the customer, discuss overall strategy, team member roles in the presentation, key information that must be gathered and presented, speaking time allotments, dress code, and any critical areas to stress or avoid.

The sales team should arrive on-time and together at the customer location. Arriving ten minutes before the scheduled time allows for last-minute meeting planning and personal thought-gathering. Early arrival—by definition—eliminates lateness. Apologies are no way to start a meeting.

Support fellow team members with smiles and gentle nods as they present to the customer. Discretely signal when it's time to wrap up or move on to the next presenter. Don't try to initiate a round of applause between speaker transitions. If the customer claps first, follow suit, but leading the charge is equivalent to holding up a sign saying, "Aren't we great?!"

Beware the Sales Expert

Salespeople must be knowledgeable in many areas, but beware of coming across to the customer as an infallible expert on all aspects of your industry. Three problems in presenting as an expert are:

1. The customer may be a self-described expert also, and—like Old West towns with two sheriffs—most meetings are too small for two experts on the same topic. Competing for expertise with the customer is poor form.

Suggestion: Up front, ask the customer about their level of expertise in the subject area, and adjust your presentation accordingly.

2. The customer may be a relative novice in the subject, and will fail to understand the technical language—acronyms, jargon, abbreviations—you use.

Suggestion: When using industry-specific jargon, occasionally pause and politely ask if the customer is familiar with the term. If they are familiar, they'll be happy to interject with their own high level of knowledge. If they're not familiar, they'll appreciate your concern about their understanding.

3. Focusing on dispensing expert testimony may preclude the salesperson from pausing, breathing, and noticing how the customer is responding...or not responding.

Suggestion: Even if the customer is eagerly nodding their head, remember that some customers eagerly nod their head and mutter, "Uh-huh," even though they may not understand, or agree with, what you are saying. Take the time every minute or two to stop the presentation and ask a question of the customer, or to ask for their feedback and opinions.

The Customer Hears You with Their Eyes

Non-verbal communication is everything you do, besides emitting words, in a presentation. This includes the way you emit your words. Paying attention to the way you present, in addition to the words you choose, will reward you with increased connection and mindshare with the customer.

Poor non-verbal communication is damaging to an otherwise good presentation. If the customer is distracted by your use, or lack, of certain mannerisms, they will hear even less of the message you are attempting to deliver.

When presenting, pay attention to how you are dressed, how you move, how you speak, where you look and how you smile. Examining each element in detail:

How you are dressed:

Fashion editors have said for years that it is better to overdress for an occasion than to under-dress. This is good advice for salespeople. Don't go overboard, however. Wearing a suit and tie when selling to an always-casual surfboard company may place distance between you and the customer before you say a word. When in doubt, telephone the company's receptionist and ask how the typical visiting salesperson dresses. When the presentation is in your company's office, dress as well as possible. Also, self-confidence is boosted when dressing well.

How you move:

Try to maintain good body posture, as customers tend to view salespeople who slouch or speak with their hands in their pockets as less effective than those who stand erect and use their hands as they speak. If you are speaking behind a lectern, don't hide behind it or hold on to it with both hands. Presenters with a smaller stature may have to be more visually active than their taller peers.

Be aware of nervous gestures, because the customer will shift their attention to your nervousness, and away from your presentation. Make gestures natural and enhancing to the presentation. Speak with your entire body, especially the arms. Avoid crossed arms, hands in pockets, and hands clasped in front or behind. See how it feels to use open arms, palms up, inclusive, inviting gestures. Video-recording a practice presentation is helpful. Review the recording with the sound off to focus on your movements.

How you speak:

A loud volume is better than speaking too softly, but don't be too loud. A fast rate of speech is better than speaking too slowly, but don't speak too fast. One problem some salespeople have is the use of "Uh" and "Um." To lessen these distracting, annoying, monotone fillers, you must first notice them. A colleague can help by clicking their pen or by making a slight movement whenever you use "Uh" or "Um." Choose, in advance, an object in the far upper corner of the room, and focus on that object whenever you sense an "Uh" or "Um" coming on. Look at the object and silently pause, resisting the urge to "Uh." After awhile you'll train yourself to substitute presidential-sounding pauses in your speech without the help of a distant focus object.

Pauses in your presentation have value, even when they're not needed as devices to avoid saying "Uh." Pauses place emphasis on what you just said, they allow information to sink in, and they enable the customer to break in with a question.

If either you or your customer speaks English as a second language, then take some extra to time make sure you are understood. Do this in a way that will not be seen as condescending.

Where you look:

Use eye contact to hold the customer's attention during your presentation, and also to gauge their level of agreement and understanding. When presenting to one person, use common sense and cultural norms to dictate the amount of appropriate eye contact. After looking away, re-establish eye contact shortly to ensure the customer is paying attention. Remember that customers' attention wanders frequently.

When presenting to a group, try to establish — and consistently re-establish — eye contact with everyone, or at least as many people as possible. When presenting to a group of tough-to-connect-with customers, find the one who is holding your gaze or nodding the most, and give that person extra one-on-one attention. Others may see this and vie for your visual attention too.

How you smile:

Be genuine with facial expressions, unless you naturally wear a scowl. Even natural scowls can be mistaken for scorn by the customer. Smiling is attractive universally, so smile as often as possible. If the topic turns so serious that smiling is inappropriate, use your face to express true solemnity. Use a mirror at home to see your various smiles, and try to use only those that feel authentic. A popular and true observation is that the warmest smiles begin with the eyes.

Handling Stress While Presenting

Some stress is not particularly harmful. The kind of pre-presentation or pre-phone call stress that causes the heart to beat slightly faster, or the palms to sweat, is normal and harmless. Such low levels of stress actually help you do better during presentations. Your body is in *alert mode,* you are aware of everything going on around you, and you appear more energized.

Repetition of the tasks that cause stress, such as a presenting or a cold calling, helps to lessen stress over time. If you haven't delivered it before, practice your presentation in advance, several times if necessary. You'll see an improvement in your confidence level and tone of voice as it becomes more familiar. Have coworkers assess your strong and weak points. Offer to return the favor to them whenever they need it. Practice doesn't necessarily make perfect, but it reduces performance stress.

Take steps to relieve stress before and during a customer presentation or phone call. Some techniques involve deep breathing and pre-presentation meditation. Other techniques involve simple tricks, such as imagining the audience dressed only in their underwear.

Preparation notwithstanding, unexpected things will happen. You may stammer with difficulty trying to say a particular word. You may trip on a power cord. You may spill your cup of water on the table. Immediately remember the Zen principle of sameness with the customer. Your audience doesn't want to see you in pain, but they do want to see how you'll handle the embarrassing situation. Don't ignore what just happened. Stop your presentation for a few seconds, smile or chuckle at yourself, and look at the others in the room to briefly acknowledge—preferably with a joke—what happened. Then move right back to the presentation.

Adroit handling of mistakes will strengthen bonds with customers.

Worth a Smile

If you need some snappy comebacks for presentation gaffes, develop your own in advance, or consider these:

- After stammering over a word, say, *"Easy for me to say."*
- After tripping on a cord, say, *"That was my Jerry Lewis impression."*
- After spilling a glass of water, say, *"Just watering the table."*

Before you begin your presentation, imagine it being a success. Imagine seeing the customers' nodding heads and smiling faces as you begin to speak. Imagine feeling confident and on-a-roll as you reach the mid-point of your presentation. Imagine concluding powerfully, knowing that your message was completely understood. Imagine hearing the customer respond positively to your call-to-action. With those images in mind, take a deep breath, smile and begin. For some salespeople, presenting to customers is the epitome of being in-the-moment.

If They Say "No Thanks"

Without a doubt, at the conclusion of some of your sales presentations, the customer will say, "Well, thanks for the information, but we're not interested at this time." Hearing their lack of interest may be surprising, especially if you thought the presentation went well.

If you are surprised at the customer's rejection of your product, take the time to reflect on whether or not you did a good enough job in qualifying the prospect or customer before the presentation. Be honest with yourself. Time is a valuable asset to a salesperson, and spending an hour or more on a presentation that failed to elicit buying interest may indicate a poor decision to present in the first place. Perhaps an extended telephone conference call would have been a better investment of your time. Ask yourself what signals you may have missed prior to the presentation. Welcome the opportunity to learn from mistakes and to avoid a similar situation in the future.

Does the customer's negative response mean the sale is lost? Probably, but not necessarily. The time you've invested in your presentation means you are entitled to a little more information from the customer before you part company. This information gathering assumes you've been paying attention to the customer's reactions, questions and comments during your presentation.

First, show the customer that you won't be *drawing swords* as a result of their lack of interest. You just want to ask a few final questions. Reacting in an adversarial manner to an initial objection will hurt the chances of ever selling to that customer.

Ask why your presentation did not interest them. Encourage honest, straightforward reasons. Let the customer speak without interruptions, and resist the temptation to object to their viewpoints.

Let them know that you understand their objections. Then, in a resigned tone of voice that genuinely reflects your disappointment (and also lessens the appearance of a contest), inquire with a question that can't be answered with a simple "Yes" or "No." Be prepared to follow-up your first question with another, if given the opportunity.

An example of such a question is: "What is your primary reason for staying with your current supplier?"

The range of possible answers is endless, but assume the customer's answer is, "Our company has an agreement with MediPlastic to buy all of our widgets from them over the next year. Maybe after the agreement expires we can speak again about your product." This is your opportunity to explore, through the use of Socratic-style, clarifying follow-up questions — not objecting statements — the alternatives:

- Ask: "Have such agreements ever been broken or modified?" If so, then, "For what reason?"

- Ask: "Are such agreements required by your department, or by the finance department?" (The question may identify previously unknown influencers on the organizational chart.)
- Ask: "What will MediPlastic demand if you break the agreement?" Then, "Is that consequence worth losing the advantages of moving to a better product at a better price?"
- Ask: "Would you consider testing our product now so that when the agreement expires you have the option of quickly moving forward?"

The object of this clarifying dialog with the customer is a two-way exchange of ideas that may motivate the customer to explore other ways to improve their business. It also uncovers information—such as the identity of other decision makers—that may be useful.

Sometimes technical objections are raised when the real problem is lack of budget. Sometimes the reverse is true.

Budgetary objections are common, and simpler than technical objections to deal with. Prepare for budgetary objections in advance. Know the various financing, leasing and payment options available. Investigate trade-in allowances. Discuss incentives such as product training or upgrades that you can provide at little or no cost to the customer.

Technical objections are more difficult. "We see your product as inferior," is best answered by possessing comprehensive information about your competitors' products, plus knowledge of the customer's beliefs and biases...the latter being the toughest to gather. A side-by-side test lab or *bake-off*, fully funded and prepared by you, is an excellent way to refute the customer's perception of your product's technical inferiority.

If the customer's objections appear invalid, stay calm and cool. Customers often have hidden agendas that cause salespeople to feel misunderstood and ineffective. If your honesty isn't reciprocated in kind, so be it. You tried your best.

When it's clear the customer wants you to stop talking and leave, depart graciously, giving sincere thanks for their time. Don't insist on scheduling follow-up communication at this sensitive point. No harm exists in gently offering quarterly new product updates, but the customer has the right to say, "Please don't. I'll call you if I need more information."

If it's clear after the presentation that no sale will result, ask the customer for their help. Before you leave, ask for the names of three of their industry acquaintances or peers whom you may call to inquire about their possible need for your company's products. Asking for this help immediately following the customer's rejection of your products is the best time. Calling or emailing your request for this information later is not as effective. (A similar method involving asking for help is described in *Chapter Five: The Zen of Prospecting*.)

You may not receive three, but even one or two new leads means that a lost opportunity may translate into a potential win elsewhere.

After the presentation, you must decide whether or not to further pursue the customer who told you, "No thanks." Pursuing a lost cause is a waste of time that robs from your ability to sell to others. If you decide to pursue, have a good reason, then create a new strategy that clearly addresses the customer's objections.

Sometimes Presentations Go Wrong

When a customer becomes disrespectful or angry during your presentation, it is important to realize that their ire is likely directed at your company and what you represent, and not at you. Even if the anger seems personal, try to see things from the customer's perspective. They may have had poor experiences with your company or another company salesperson in the past. They may have had customer service, support, shipping or billing issues with your company. The customer may simply be having a bad day. They may be ill, or they may have a child or loved one who is sick. Or they may have personal problems, such as money trouble, substance addictions or personality disorders.

To deal with an angry customer, leave your ego at the door and maintain a poised, professional manner. A salesperson should never lose their temper in front of a customer.

Of all of the tests of a Zen mind, the greatest may be dealing with another's anger. Attempt to maintain *some* connection with the person, even though the connection may seem already broken. Give the dialogue a chance to resolve itself into one that is constructive, not destructive.

To do this, allow the customer to speak freely, without interruption, even if you are itching to jump in with a rebuttal. When they are finished speaking, thank the customer for voicing their concern, and repeat back to the customer a summary of their remarks. For example, "I appreciate that. So, if I understand you correctly . . ." The customer may choose to refine their remarks at that point.

Answer the customer's concerns completely, addressing all points raised. Avoid saying, "I hope that answers your question," when you are finished. If the customer becomes even angrier, find the best way — or at least some way — to agree with them:

- "I agree with [all or part] of your point of view."

- "I agree that things appear the way you describe."

- "I agree that you have a right to your point of view."

If you are correct and the customer is wrong, use a gentle-but-firm voice and say so. If the customer is correct, admit fault and thank them for helping you correct the problem. When follow-ups are required for problem resolution, create a timeline, stick to it, and give progress reports to the customer.

After such a difficult presentation, find some private space and take the time needed to re-center yourself. Consider the meditation below. Calming your mind and letting go of the customer's potentially poisonous words will help you to productively move on with the rest of your day, without a nagging resentment.

The *Thoughts-are-Leaves* Meditation

Find a quiet location and sit comfortably. Visualize yourself as sitting alone on the soft, grassy bank of a bubbling brook or a gently flowing stream. See the current moving the water from right to left. *The stream represents your meditation.* It is a warm, autumn day, and you feel peaceful and connected with nature.

Visualize a large oak tree directly across the bank of the stream, towering above you. *The oak tree represents your mind.* The tree's branches hold thousands of big, golden leaves. *The leaves represent your thoughts.*

Visualize each new thought as an oak leaf detaching from a branch and falling slowly downward to the stream in front of you. It lands in the moving water with a small splash and is carried away, out of your sight, and out of your mind.

Look at the thought/leaf and accept it as being what it is. Not good or bad, just a thought. Sometime after the current of the stream carries off the first thought/leaf, another will fall from the tree. Let this thought/leaf go, just as the first, without judgment.

The objective is to clear your mind of interrupting thoughts and to experience an emptiness into which pureness and wisdom and contentment will flow. Do not try to clear your mind. Instead, focus on full, deep inhalations of breath, and even longer exhalations. Silently counting the seconds you inhale ("1, 2, 3, 4") and exhale ("1, 2, 3, 4, 5, 6") helps.

Thoughts will enter your mind, such as, "Is this meditation working?" "How much time has gone by?" and "What is on my agenda this afternoon?" Let each thought fall into the water and drift away.

The moments in between thoughts/leaves falling are supremely special moments. Enjoy your inner silence and peacefulness. Appreciate the calmness.

Be patient with this meditation. Do it for only a few minutes at first, then gradually expand to five or ten minutes.

Lessons from a Zen Sage

"Your mind is like the sea. When the wind comes, there are very big waves. When the wind dies down, the waves become smaller and smaller, until finally the wind disappears altogether and the sea is like clear mirror, reflecting the mountains and the trees and all things."

Zen Master Seung Sahn, *Three Letters to a Beginner*, Kwan Um School of Zen, 1987

"Words and magic were in the beginning one and the same thing, and even today words retain much of their magical power."
- Sigmund Freud

7
THE ZEN OF MANAGING SALESPEOPLE

(Executive staff and sales staff can benefit from this chapter too.)

Lessons from a Zen Sage

"Defeatism, apathy, cynicism, despair…these are invoked by the few who do better when the world is managed badly, and when the many are prevented from demanding and implementing good management."
Robert A.F. Thurman, Ph.D.[12]

Leading by Example

The chasm between managing and managing well is wide and deep. To manage is to lead employees. To manage well is to lead employees ethically, effectively, and without arrogance. Company owners, executives and managers must set the highest examples of attitude and conduct for employees. Some companies, including IBM, HP, Proctor & Gamble and Motorola, consistently have a top-down approach to leadership by example. These companies are good corporate citizens with excellent records in areas such as:

- The environment: pollution reduction, recycling and energy-saving measures

- Community relations: philanthropy, foundations, community service, outreach and scholarships

- Employee relations: fair wages, paid benefits, family-oriented policies and parental leave

- Diversity: utilization of minorities, women, the disabled and veterans

- Customer relations: quality management programs and focus on customer satisfaction.

It's clear to see that such corporate attitude and behavior is far more than merely operating within the boundaries of the law. Legal compliance is a *lowest bar* exercise that focuses on avoiding culpability, fines or prosecution. Being a positive example to employees, customers and even other companies is the truest form of excellent management. Reach for a higher bar.

The Powerful Role of Ethics

A broad definition of ethics is: *Individual, organizational or cultural beliefs about what is right and wrong, good and bad, in actions that affect others.* This definition can be extended to include the rules and standards that govern the actions of an individual, organization or culture.

The difference between morals and ethics is clarified by considering morals as principles of right and wrong conduct, and ethics as a system of morally correct conduct. The principles you live by are morals, and the system by which you act on those principles is ethics.

Words from the Wise
"You can easily judge the character of a man by how he treats those who can do nothing for him."
Johann Wolfgang von Goethe, 1749-1832, German poet, novelist and philosopher

In Zen, as in many philosophies, determining ethical behavior involves examination of whether or not the action or speech in question is likely harmful to yourself or another. If it is, avoid that behavior. The Bible's *Golden Rule* — along with related 'ethics of reciprocity' in most other religions — is a similar instruction. Such decision making is the mark of a disciplined, mindful person.

Your inner voice is often the best guide when confronted with difficult decisions and situations. The development and adoption of personal ethics must come from inside you, but ethical understanding comes from lessons derived from external sources.

The process of applying ethics when choosing how to act must be applied in equal measure at home, at work and all places in between. Ethics, like Zen, knows no time clock. The application of the same set of ethical principles to both personal and professional actions makes choices far easier than wondering which of several sets of principles should be applied.

Throughout the day a manager will refer to their single ethical standard many times, depending on the role they are playing. When in a professional role, such as manager, peer or subordinate, ethical actions will include:

- Objectivity and impartiality
- Sincerity and disclosure
- Privacy and discretion
- Responsibility and sense of duty
- Avoidance of conflict of interest.

When in a personal role, such as family member or friend, ethical actions will include:

- Concern for the welfare of others
- Respect for the individualism of others
- Trustworthiness and honesty
- Not taking unfair advantage
- Kindness, generosity, and doing good
- Preventing harm.

Words from the Wise
"The first step in the evolution of ethics is a sense of solidarity with other human beings."
Dr. Albert Schweitzer, 1875-1965, Nobel Prize-winning surgeon and theologian

---

Managing Salespeople Ethically

Important duties of the sales manager are motivating and mentoring. A well managed team does well, and feels good about how they accomplished the task. A poorly managed team may do well in spurts, but over the long term they'll fail, and they'll know that they could have done better.

Leading ethically by example requires effective communications for the team to understand what is acceptable, desired and expected behavior. Communication is a two-way street that flows between manager and salesperson. If either direction of the communication flow is blocked, sales revenue will suffer, as will relationships internal to the organization.

The temptations to stretch ethical behavior in sales are everywhere:

- Maximization of profit
- Cost cutting
- Expansion of market share
- Short-term revenue reporting.

Managers who establish, exhibit and maintain a firm stance concerning ethical selling must overcome these temptations. Executive-level management must be the first to demonstrate — and the last to enforce — proper codes of conduct. Enforcement should start with low-level management and work upward when necessary.

The toughest decisions for managers are those that involve two alternate courses of action, both of which have ethical attributes, and neither of which is the clear answer. The ability to officiate such predicaments is the mark of an excellent manager. From time to time even the best manager will fail to act ethically. It's human nature. Learning from mistakes is how progress is made.

Words from the Wise

"... The more emotionally healthy executives, as measured on a battery of tests, the more likely they were to score high on ethics tests."
Wall Street Journal, April 11th 1991

The modern business of selling, and business in general, reflects the improvements that organizational-level ethical codes of conduct have made over the last one hundred years. A century ago, children were forced to work at young ages and for extended hours. Price fixing was common between similar businesses. Employees had few if any rights, and were fired for capricious reasons. Managers could freely intimidate and harass employees. Many improvements had to be impelled by new laws, but — with exceptions — law generally reflects the current will of the people.

Using legal compliance as the lowest denominator for decision-making is hardly ethical behavior, although having in place an organizational doctrine on ethics has legal benefits. With properly written, published and disseminated ethical codes of conduct, an organization risks less if an employee creates a criminal or civil problem because of poor ethical behavior. Even Federal Sentencing Guidelines note that corporate fines may be lessened if violations occur contrary to such codes of conduct being in place and enforced.

Beyond legal, public image, or other justifications, managing ethically is simply the right way to manage.

In Management We Trust

The level of trust within a sales organization should reflect the level of trust that the company itself solicits from customers. If customers are encouraged to put their complete trust in the product, then internal teams must do the same with each other. It's management's job to guide that internal process.

Trust in a sales organization flows back and forth, between all involved entities: salesperson, customer, coworker, manager and subordinate. Trust involves believing that the person to whom you disclose personal or sensitive information, or with whom you engage in an act of mutual reliance, will safely handle their responsibility, and will not harm you physically, emotionally or financially.

Managers building a sales team that trusts—and relies upon— each other must take these responsibilities seriously. It takes time to build trust, and, once built, trust must be carefully maintained. Trust is a fragile thing. If metaphorically dropped, it shatters, and repaired trust is never as strong as the original.

A 2003 article in *The Harvard Business Review* stated:

"Researchers have established that trust is critical to organizational effectiveness. Being trustworthy yourself, however, does not guarantee that you are capable of building trust in an organization. That takes old-fashioned managerial virtues like consistency, clear communication, and a willingness to tackle awkward questions. It also requires a good defense: You must protect trust from its enemies. Any act of bad management erodes trust. Among the most common enemies of trust are:

- *Inconsistent messages from top management*
- *Inconsistent standards*
- *A willingness to tolerate incompetence or bad behavior*
- *Dishonest feedback*
- *A failure to trust others to do good work*
- *A tendency to ignore painful or politically charged situations*
- *Consistent corporate underperformance*
- *Rumors."*[13]

An increase in trust is a reduction in risk and uncertainty, which in turn will keep sales team functions flowing smoothly. Relationships will form and strengthen, and team members will increasingly value those trusting relationships, taking whatever steps necessary to preserve them.

Management must ensure that support or ancillary personnel not directly tied to the core sales team, yet occasionally involved in the selling process, are held to the same high standards. Such support personnel include those involved in shipping, support, maintenance, billing and legal departments.

Another advantage of running a high-trust organization is the level of internal flexibility and creativity. Instead of being constantly monitored, the person to whom a task is assigned can accomplish it the best way possible. The outcome is never in doubt because of the trust the team shares.

The test of trust is in the sum of the answers to these three questions:

1) Are the communications reliable?
2) Are the actions consistent?
3) Are the outcomes desirable?

Communicating Clearly

Good managers communicate effectively. Effectiveness and precision doesn't mean inflexibility, merely a clarity and brevity to all oral and written communications. Employees receiving such precise communication will sense—without respect to the content of the message—that management is efficient, which will spur employees to conduct themselves in kind.

Orient yourself to your staff when composing and delivering a communication. Take yourself out of the picture, if possible, and construct messages that resonate with your employees, based upon their roles and their goals. As you communicate, consider how your message will be received. Five staff members will receive the same message five different ways, so be open to—and be prepared for—feedback and discussion. Communicating non-negotiable edicts is sometimes a duty of sales management, yet firmness doesn't exclude dialogue.

Respect your staff's time, and don't keep them waiting when you have asked them to meet with you. Time is the biggest constraint for management, but the same is true for salespeople. Your wasting of their time as they wait outside your office conveys the message that your time is more valuable than is theirs. Such an attitude hovers between mere arrogance and outright disrespect.

Exercise #13: List management duties that you wish more salespeople appreciated or knew about

- _____
- _____
- _____
- _____
- _____

Empowering Through Positive Reinforcement

Sales managers who direct salespeople without empowering them are managing inefficiently, and are working far harder than they have to. Empowering salespeople builds their confidence, develops their character, and teaches them how to motivate themselves.

Empowerment isn't always easy to accomplish. Sales managers must first guide the individual toward seeing the advantages of being fueled from within. Although motivation can come from inside or outside the individual, the most successful salespeople are self-motivated.

Salespeople are a diverse group, and each individual responds to different motivations. Motivation is either positive (reward-based) or negative (fear-based). Decades of research have proven that the positive kind works best. Ruling with the proverbial iron fist is suitable only for sales managers who, for some reason, prefer an environment filled with fear and insecurity.

There remain corporate cultures that still encourage or require heavy-handed sales management techniques. Effective, ethical managers will either leave such organizations, or they will insulate their staff and focus on building trusting relationships. Management by intimidation is best suited for military boot camp, in which the goal is to strip away individuality in preparation for a new mindset. Even in the military, however, such a management style becomes unproductive soon after boot camp.

Shunning negative, fear-based management does not mean embracing a utopian, praise-every-little-thing style. Empowering, positive management means acknowledging salespeople for accomplishing key steps in the selling process, including:

- A productive telephone prospecting session that results in appointments

- A customer meeting that results in progress toward a sale

- Overcoming a competitive threat that endangered a sale

- Closing a sale.

If a salesperson is working hard on a big deal that hasn't yet closed, avoid the temptation to comment, "I need you to close that one to help the district number." Salespeople know perfectly well how important each sale is, to themselves and to the district. Superfluous pressure is counterproductive. Consider instead, "I really appreciate the hard work you're putting into this one. Keep it up." The message has no hidden meaning or agenda, which keeps the salesperson focused and productive without invoking fear. Follow up by offering your time and ideas on ways to help the stalled deal move forward.

The same acknowledgment approach is helpful when you *catch* employees making progress through a strenuous telephone prospecting session, or organizing a business lunch with a key client. "Good job!" goes a long way to making salespeople feel appreciated and respected. Pats on the back are underrated.

For outstanding behavior, reward salespeople in outstanding fashion. A simple "attaboy" (or "attagirl") is fine for the little stuff, but consider a $25 gift certificate for an employee who is complimented by a customer because they, "...went the extra mile." Other confidence-building rewards include a monthly or quarterly top performer trophy or plaque, and an end-of-year holiday trip for the best of the best.

Non-tangible rewards are sometimes more effective than tangible ones. Conventional wisdom holds that salespeople are mainly motivated by money. Yet, for many, recognition is highly prized. Recognition in front of peers makes everyone feel good. During team meetings or conference calls, consider regularly pointing out the *best practices* behavior of certain individuals. When dealing with executive management, fight the temptation to take credit for a big win that was attributable to the work of a team member. Make sure that particular salesperson knows that the top brass is well aware of their individual accomplishment. Many reps value such executive recognition far more than a gift certificate.

Rewards for excellence will create internal comparisons—and possibly sniping behavior—between salespeople. While some competition is always healthy, make clear that your focus is on an individual performing to the best of their ability, not besting others. To avoid excessive internal comparisons, discover what truly motivates each salesperson. Commit team member motivations to memory or write them down, then help each team member to achieve their individual goals.

A salesperson with clear personal goals operates with a *personalized mental carrot* as their focus. This makes it easier for them to identify and eliminate activity that doesn't move them closer to their goals. Guiding employees toward a self-help mindset is the ultimate in empowerment.

Hiring Well

Hiring qualified, competent salespeople is always a challenge for the sales manager. Compatibility between the new hire and the existing sales team—or the corporate culture—is often overlooked. The best salesperson for one company may be unsuitable for another. Take the time to speak with, and interview, as many candidates as possible before filling an open position. As attractive as "getting it over with" sounds, the hiring process seldom has shortcuts.

The quickest way to hire a suitable candidate is through a personal reference to a competitor's top-performing salesperson, ideally one dissatisfied with their current employer and actively seeking employment elsewhere. Recruiters can help. Uncover the reasons for their dissatisfaction. Verify information from other sources. Hiring a problematic salesperson away from a competitor is doing a favor for the other company.

Qualification is as important in hiring a new salesperson as it is in the prospecting phase of selling. If someone doesn't seem right for the job, keep looking. Putting the wrong candidate into an open position has ripple effects that will negatively affect sales revenue, the sales team, the customer, and possibly even your job.

Besides applicable industry experience and technical skills, the top qualities to look for in candidates are:

- Excellent communications skills and ability to work well in a team environment

- Ability to self-motivate and take initiative, plus a high degree of personal integrity and ethics

- Ability to lead and motivate others

- Ability to adapt to change.

Even though the hiring manager will have the final word, have at least one or two other sales team members interview the candidate, ideally on the same day the hiring manager interviews them. Two reasons for this are:

1) Gathering a multifaceted view of the candidate's abilities produces a clearer picture to be discussed internally after the candidate leaves.

2) The candidate is able to evaluate their level of interest after viewing the environment in which—and the people with whom—they may work.

Screen the candidate's resume for accuracy. Reference checking educational claims is a simple matter of contacting schools and verifying graduation status and dates. A lie about education may indicate other lies on the resume. Employment history should be checked, but prior employers are reluctant to release more than dates of employment. Calling resume-listed references is necessary, but will likely result in mostly positive reviews.

When interviewing, use probing, clarifying questions about personal goals, stories of biggest sales wins and losses, and reasons for leaving jobs. Encourage humor and mild digression in the conversation. Uncover as much information as possible. After the interview is over, if you decide you have additional questions, call the candidate for the answers.

Once the ideal candidate is hired, the orientation process becomes critical. Intense, one-on-one manager/salesperson training sessions are valuable when combined with ride-alongs with current—preferably senior—sales team members. Let the new salesperson see the different faces and selling styles in your company. This will encourage their unique personality to shine through. Once that occurs the new salesperson is ready to establish prospect connections and create customer relationships.

Exercise #14: List the best advice you've ever been given about managing salespeople

- _____
- _____
- _____
- _____
- _____

Friendship Between Manager and Salesperson

Personal friendships will occasionally develop between the manager and certain salespeople. Like it or not, there exists a power difference in such a friendship. As the friendship develops, be sure that both parties realize that the manager's duty is to sometimes make tough decisions regarding personnel, up to and including termination.

For the manager, subordinate friendships may be fulfilling, but work-related disagreements sometimes damage the relationship. The opposite reaction—not properly managing a subordinate because of friendship—can be equally deleterious. If both parties clearly understand the dual roles they play, there will be few misunderstandings and hurt feelings.

Salespeople Just Wanna Have Fun

Make work as fun as possible and you'll see happier, more-productive salespeople. Many perks from the non-sales world, such as four-day work weeks (ten-hour days), do not translate well into the sales profession. You need salespeople available to speak with customers five days a week...more if you sell on weekends. Another corporate benefit that doesn't translate well into sales is *casual day*. Sales staff with customer face-to-face contact must adhere to your industry's typical attire. Customers understand casual Fridays, but they still expect a certain dress code from salespeople with whom they meet.

Worth a Smile

"All I wanna do is have some fun; I get a feeling I'm not the only one."
A&M recording artist Sheryl Crow

Sales-centric, stress-relieving perks include providing work-out or relaxation facilities close to—perhaps even inside—the office. For small sales offices, consider contributing $30 per month for local gym membership fees. Salespeople may then exercise locally, which minimizes their morning or afternoon rush-hour commute. One of the nicest conveniences in an office is a refrigerator stocked with no-charge soft drinks, and a nearby tray with chips and healthy snacks. If funds are low, consider an honor-bar system.

Flexible working hours for salespeople with small children at home shows genuine compassion and appreciation. If telecommuting and home-offices make sense, set guidelines and monitor the results.

A great way to keep things light-hearted is to schedule monthly fun events for salespeople and support staff. Bowling is always good for a laugh. Entertainment arcades with team activities such as group video game or race car contests bring out the competitive spirit. Have a stash of token give-away gifts for the winners, but ensure everyone walks away with something.

Limit alcohol use during these fun outings. A drink or two is fine, but managers and their companies who provide unlimited consumption that contributes to drunk driving accidents may be held partially liable.

A group of salespeople laughing and high five-ing each other during such an event will perform better as individuals and team members at work the next day. Anything to improve the team spirit and the we're-all-in-this-together attitude is money well spent.

Teaching Time Management

Teaching efficiency, especially time management, is a key area in which sales managers can positively coach their staff.

Applying industry averages, for a salesperson trying to sell a product that costs $50,000, of ten prospects telephoned only one will result in an appointment. One in four prospect appointments ends up as a potential sale, and only one in four potential sales ends up in an actual sale. The bottom line: for a company that assigns a relatively low (for such high-cost products) two million dollar per year quota, the salesperson must secure 640 prospect appointments per year, resulting in 160 potential sales, which in turn should result in 40 sales closed. That's three appointments per day, in addition to taking the time to perform new prospect calling, to manage existing customers, and to participate in sales meetings, trainings and all other company-required activities.

Precious little time is available to conduct those customer appointments. In a study conducted by Irwin / McGraw-Hill, it was discovered that in the typical workweek, a salesperson only spends 31% of their time selling face-to-face with the customer.[14] Phone selling, waiting/traveling, and administrative tasks take up 25%, 18% and 15% of the salesperson's time, respectively. That leaves 2½ hours of each 8-hour day to actually meet with customers.

Managers should coach their salespeople in:

- Qualifying the difference between high-probability and low-probability prospects.
- Anticipating and replying to prospect objections.
- Quickly moving forward initial conversations into formal presentations.
- Utilizing existing tools to eliminate *reinventing the wheel*.
- Maximizing customer face time and minimizing administrative tasks.

Exercise #15: List current or past subordinates who have thanked you for helping in their sales career

- _____
- _____
- _____
- _____
- _____

The Self-Absorbed Salesperson

Some salespeople suffer from healthy self-respect being carried to the extreme...self-absorption. A salesperson's role is to sell products and generate revenue. Unfortunately, when the primary message heard is, "What's in it for me?" as opposed to, "What can I do for you?" the customer will rightly turn a deaf ear.

Self-absorbed salespeople are often rude and impatient in public settings such as restaurants. Other traits include:

- They love to hear themselves talk, but they dislike listening to others
- They are often late for meetings, and they dismiss their lateness with a chuckle

- They are visibly upset when others are late, or others make mistakes
- They see their logic and viewpoints as flawless, and those of others as flawed.

Self-absorbed salespeople are sometimes mistakenly identified as *real go-getters* because of their propensity to comment upon and know about seemingly everything.

While prospecting, a self-absorbed salesperson may be able to initially hide their arrogance. When the customer realizes that the salesperson is impatiently waiting for their turn to talk, and not really listening, the customer may lose interest too. The self-absorbed salesperson who conversationally fails with a customer will often later denigrate the person as unintelligent or unqualified.

The self-absorbed salesperson is tough to guide and manage. Before full-scale critique and correction takes place, initiate a guidance/education process. Schedule a discussion with the individual in which your goal will be to deliver a message in a gentle yet effective manner. Before the discussion, consider what your strategy will be. It may be as simple as showing alternate active listening techniques that will help the salesperson achieve more success.

Conduct discussions in private, to avoid potential ego bruising if others hear. Choose your words carefully. Discuss the work, and not the person. Instead of focusing on what they're doing wrong, focus on new ways to achieve the things that motivate them.

Use a suggestive tone, as opposed to an authoritative tone. For example, "In my experience, I've found that honing in on every word the customer is saying—and fighting the urge to jump in too quickly—really helps to move the selling process along faster and easier."

Encourage the salesperson to discuss their professional goals with you. Then tie together your suggestions with their goals. The best outcome of such a discussion is to have the self-absorbed salesperson describe which new methods they are willing to try to achieve greater success. Words that come from your mouth won't have as much effect as those that come from the salesperson's. End the discussion on an up note, an encouraging pat on the back and a smile.

If, after time, it appears that gentle guidance is not working, more direct measures must be taken.

Coaching, Correcting and Critiquing

Managing a sales team has many similarities to coaching a sports team. When the team wins, the individual contributors can and should take the credit. When the team fails, the manager or coach can and should take the blame. Humility plays a large part in ethical, effective management.

A sales manager's primary responsibility is to hire, train and develop individuals that will achieve specific objectives set by executive management. Development includes providing tools and resources. Development also includes coaching, correcting and critiquing individual behavior. This counseling function is one of the toughest aspects of sales leadership.

No single, best way exists to critique and correct all salespeople. An effective sales manager leading a team of ten salespeople must develop ten ways of delivering critical advice and counseling them on metrics, methodologies and expected results.

Critiquing often involves hurt feelings, so prepare for expressions of emotion. It's common to witness anger, justification, blame, frustration, defeatism and personal revelations. Listen and sympathize appropriately, but end critical conversations with an unambiguous statement of measurable expectation. Set, and keep to, a schedule of follow-up meetings until the correction has been accomplished.

Salespeople should be given every opportunity to succeed. Before initiating any termination action, clearly and repeatedly detail the job's expectations and objectives to the salesperson. When critiques and corrections lead to reprimands and warnings, be sure to accurately record the results of manager-salesperson meetings. Consult your company's human resources department every step of the way.

From time to time sales managers will have no alternative but to terminate the employment of a salesperson. When that time comes, carry out the task with complete dignity for the affected employee. Keep the termination meeting short and formal, without adding useless comments such as, "You know, I was fired once, back in..." The fired employee is in emotional turmoil, and doesn't care for gratuitous sympathy. Ensure all papers signed, and all statements you make—including promises for post-termination references and assistance—are in strict compliance with company legal policy.

Don't rush to fill the opening. Pause to reflect on the causes of the failure. Look closely at yourself, not just at the actions of the terminated employee. Make necessary adjustments in your outlook and objectives before the next hire.

Termination may reflect poorly on the hiring manager. If the terminated salesperson was initially qualified in key areas such as interpersonal skills, plus industry, product, geographical and competitive knowledge—in other words a *good hire*—then the termination was likely the result of either:

- A change in the personal situation of the salesperson outside of the influence of the sales manager, or

- The lack of proper motivation and guidance by the sales manager.

Without seeking to blame, objective examination of the causes of the termination is important for both the sales manager and the employee. It's possible for both to learn something of value from such a negative experience.

Managing With a Beginner's Mind

Scientists who perform experiments keep an open mind to all possible results, expected or not. The unforeseen is encouraged. Zen—as a human science of the mind—approaches life with a similar outlook. *Not-knowing* and *beginner's mind* define each event that occurs during the day as an opportunity for growth. All that's required is resistance to the urge to respond to each event in a pre-determined manner.

For the manager, not-knowing is disconcerting at first. It implies throwing out pre-conceived notions and learning to react freshly to experiences, especially to familiar-looking experiences, to which you've reacted the same way for years.

Seeing events, others and yourself with a not-knowing outlook opens the mind to creative solutions. The practice and discipline involved in developing the not-knowing mind involves letting go of the expert inside you, and seeing everything through the wide-open eyes of a novice.

With a compassionate Zen mind, managers are free to focus on what's in the salesperson's best interest, as opposed to their own, and to use that knowledge to encourage and empower. A manager who is clear about what they value also understands the personalized values that drive others.

Although some managers complain about the pressures and responsibilities of leading others, developing a group of individuals into a cohesive, motivated and successful unit is immensely rewarding.

People seldom forget those who have led and managed them. The negative influence of an ineffective manager on a salesperson won't linger forever. (It may garner an occasional shake of the head or an off-color comment.) The coaching of an effective, ethical manager, however, will last a lifetime. The lessons learned will serve as an example to the salesperson—should they decide to take on a managerial role—of the positive effects that occur when a subordinate is well managed.

8
THE ZEN OF TEAM SELLING

No Lone Rangers

The concept of a team is sometimes viewed as unnecessary in the realm of selling. Salespeople may see themselves as Lone Rangers, not in need of any help, save for the occasional advice from a Tonto (or technical sales specialist).

Teams and teamwork are, of course, an integral part of selling. From the building and management of the salesperson's company, to product manufacturing and distribution, to customer service and support, nothing is accomplished alone.

The successful salesperson realizes that achievement of their individual quota relies not just on their own efforts, but on the awareness, attitudes and task execution of others...just as others rely on the same from the salesperson.

Seeing this interaction and reliance on others as a win-win scenario is the optimal viewpoint. Seeing teamwork as an irritating-but-necessary hindrance is not only sub-optimal, but is corruptive to the running of the company. Customers expect rapid, precise response from sales organizations, and a team approach is the best way to deliver that response.

Effective salespeople seem to instinctively understand the benefits of teaming. They surround themselves with a virtual team of people and resources that are instrumental in their success. Such people constantly thank those around them for their efforts, and the cycle continues with everyone involved feeling rewarded.

Win-win attitudes within interpersonal and interdepartmental teams involve:

- Clearly defined roles, expectations and organizational charts
- Fast, accurate and respectful team member communications
- Management example-setting, guidance, problem resolution and recognition.

Team dynamics are unique, depending on team size, structure and objectives. Getting in tune with—and contributing to—your team's distinctiveness is effort well spent. Be alert for attitudes and behavior that are harmful to your team, such as blocked communications, power struggles and bruised egos.

A Rapport of Non-Competition with Coworkers

Interpersonal relationships you develop with coworkers can enhance your life both on and off the job. Friendships develop when peers:

- Share tasks
- Work physically close together
- Have common interests or hobbies
- Participate in similar life events such as marriage, child rearing or buying a house.

Friendships at work are under a higher degree of pressure than friendships outside of work. Promotions, raises and lopsided success or recognition can place strain on such relationships. To mitigate strain, establish a rapport of non-competition early in the friendship. Be in mutual agreement that your closeness will not be affected by work.

Most coworkers will be acquaintances, not best friends. Protect and nurture these relationships by showing a great deal of respect for everyone, especially those on lower parts of the organization chart. Secretaries, receptionists and administrative assistants are some of the hardest working, least respected and most underpaid professionals in an organization. Take time to regularly show them how much you value their work. Buy them a lunch. Bring them some flowers. Compliment their appearance (while sensitively avoiding any suggestion of unwanted approach or harassment).

Exercise #16: List personal friendships that began as a customer/salesperson relationship

- _____
- _____
- _____
- _____
- _____

The Cost of Envy

Salespeople are often motivated by money, and seeing a coworker close a large deal, receive a big commission check and arrive at work the following week driving a new luxury car is tough to ignore. It can hurt even more to see another's success if you recently lost a big sale.

The most harmful envious reaction to a peer's sales victory is to feel—or worse, say out loud—that they didn't deserve it. The poison arrow is actually pointed at the envious, resentful one. Such feelings are cancerous to individuals and to organizations. When encountered, acknowledge these feelings for what they are. Take the time to decide how best to deal with them. Try to find ways, however uncomfortable at first, to sincerely and humbly applaud the victorious peer. When envy is felt, it's entirely up to you to decide how long—a minute, an hour, a day—you will clutch it, and when you will let it go.

When *bluebirds*—deals that fortuitously fall into a salesperson's lap—happen, remember that randomness has no favorites. When chance smiles on you, celebrate. When it smiles on others, congratulate.

Lessons from a Zen Sage

"How does it feel to be number two? Perhaps you can smile bravely, but is your heart also smiling?"
Zen Master Robert Aiken, when asked how best to introspectively deal with feelings when a coworker is happy after a success.

Envy sometimes stems from viewing peers as competitors. Such an adversarial position turns coworkers into enemies who must be defeated at any cost. When they win, you lose. To erase this negative, self-defeating viewpoint, recognize your coworkers as fellow, feeling humans with whom you are universally connected. This empathetic stance sets the stage for true compassion when your coworkers lose a deal, and true elation when they win.

Feelings of envy may make you feel shameful and ridiculous ... sometimes even ugly. Envy's lack of redeeming qualities makes it somewhat easier to deal with than more complex feelings such as desire, which can have positive and negative attributes. In the spirit of *turning lemons into lemonade*, consider transforming brief feelings of envy for a coworker into personal motivation to work harder at achieving your goals. "They did well? Darn it, I'm going to do well too!" That's about the only way the green monster of envy actually does some good.

Think Before You Hit Send

Emailing team members is a great tool for clear communications, especially when the sender is respectful of the recipient. Company email systems are efficient at disseminating information to large groups and for managing a subject thread through numerous replies and comments. Email isn't as efficient as the telephone, however, for soliciting quick responses to an urgent question. Email also makes poor communication easy, and—when the words are hurtful—can create problems at work.

Write emails in a manner that reflects how you would speak, face to face, with the recipient. If you wouldn't dare shout at a fellow employee, then "shouting" with ALL CAPS in an email to the same employee is inconsistent.

Likewise, if coworkers are busy with their work you probably won't stand in their doorway and tell them jokes. Sending unsolicited jokes via email can be similarly aggravating.

Despite its ability to accurately convey information, email has a remarkable ability to also convey misunderstandings, most of which are perpetrated by the sender, not the receiver. Paying close attention to the style in which you write emails will reap positive dividends in maintaining good relationships with coworkers.

Shield yourself from the ill will of email recipients by following these guidelines:

- Scan each outgoing email for viruses
- In the text of the email, inform the reader if the attachment is large
- Use the bcc: (blind carbon copy) option infrequently, if at all.

Long, Tedious Internal Sales Meetings

Mandatory staff meetings are an integral part of sales. No matter how bored you become in a sales meeting, know that you're probably not the only one. Hearing others speak and present for extended periods puts some people in a stupor. The best way to deal with it—not to mention the best way to come away from the meeting with the intended information—is to practice Zen mind self-awareness and to be in-the-moment as much as possible.

Sales meetings are a great opportunity to work on improving active listening skills. It's amazing how fast and how easily the mind wanders. Observing the way others present helps you see the effectiveness of various styles of non-verbal communication. Consider adopting what works for them into your tool bag of techniques. You'll also know how customers feel when a salesperson drones on for too long.

When you aren't the one presenting or speaking, try to focus on what's being said so that you can support the speaker, contribute to the conversation, and be a more valuable team member. When you are the one presenting to the sales team, remember how badly it feels to see half the room dozing, gazing elsewhere or whispering to their neighbor. Paying close, supportive attention to a coworker as they speak will inspire that coworker to do the same for you when it's your turn to speak.

In the Zen spirit of team selling, find ways in sales meetings to help your peers solve their challenges. Can you selflessly:

- Participate in their success?
- Share approaches you've used, presentations you've created and proposals you've written?
- Share lead or prospecting resources you've found?
- Share specifically-needed contacts and offer to make key introductions?

Expect nothing from your offerings, but know that such positive energy has a karmic way of going and coming around.

Watch for political oneupmanship in sales meetings. It's a tempting time and place for quick stabs and pokes at your peers' faults and lack of knowledge. Avoid the temptation. Also, if a coworker seems to constantly focus on "kissing up" to the manager, don't judge or disparage their behavior. Most managers are astute enough to recognize a sly subordinate's intentions.

Dealing With Your Sales Manager

Your sales manager is a cheerleader for your success. Your success contributes to theirs, not just in revenue terms, but from a sense of accomplishment that they hired, developed and empowered the right person.

When management directs you, they are performing the role they're being paid for, not taking advantage of their position to randomly bark orders. If you see your sales manager as unqualified, consider if you are simply unable to also see the abilities and qualifications that gave them value in the eyes of their superiors. Listen to your manager just as carefully as you listen to customers. In both instances you'll come out ahead.

Salespeople who perform well often earn more compensation than their managers. Sales managers typically won't complain about high levels of commission for their top salespeople. The best sales teams are those in which a significant number of individuals are doing well and making money.

A sales manager's job is to direct downward and report upward. Salespeople sometimes see their sales manager as an unnecessary layer. A salesperson who personally knows the sales manager's vice president may think, 'Why can't I just report directly to the VP?' The answer is that the VP cannot efficiently manage more than a handful of direct reports. Plus, a local sales manager is far better suited to deal with local issues.

The military follows the *rule of threes* which states that a corporal can effectively manage three privates, a sergeant can effectively manage three corporals, and so on up the chain of command. Sales managers can manage more than a staff of three salespeople if the balance between passive management and active management is favorable. A sales manager can passively manage—that is manage without a great deal of task-to-task direction—a maximum of ten or so direct reports. A tough job for the sales manager is managing people actively, including new, probationary and poorly performing staff. Such day-by-day—sometimes hour-by-hour—supervision will consume much of a manager's day.

Exercise #17: List the best sales managers for whom you've worked, and what made them the best

- _____
- _____
- _____
- _____
- _____

Make Yourself Easy to Manage

Ask your sales manager what _their_ manager requires from _them_. Helping your manager complete their required tasks—as long as your primary role isn't negatively affected—will help to make your job easier.

Most salespeople don't have visibility into the less glamorous aspects of their manager's job. Tasks such as collecting, analyzing and rolling up sales forecasts, spending hours in meetings and on conference calls, dealing with human resources issues and shouldering a hefty revenue commitment make many managers wonder why they left the relative calm of prospecting and selling to customers.

Conventional wisdom says that salespeople and sales management are motivated almost entirely by money. Ergo, sell a ton and the sales manager won't bug you. Not always true. Savvy sales managers view revenue as key, but they also know that salespeople who employ good selling skills will make it through a poor selling period until the good times roll once again. Time-honored good selling skills include:

- Creative prospecting

- Complete product knowledge
- Superior presentation skills
- Efficient time management
- Continuous cultivation of repeat and referral business.

Salespeople with such skills will have peaks and valleys in their revenue stream, but they don't require *management via microscope*. Conversely, salespeople closing a flurry of deals are worthy of management approval, but not to the exclusion of management's insistence that good selling skills be maintained.

From time to time sales managers will critique you, they will be disappointed in you, and they will—hopefully infrequently—be angry with you. Facing a manager's anger will often cause you to instinctively deploy stress-sensitive defense or escape mechanisms. Take a deep breath and let the manager know the way you're hearing their anger. "It sounds like you are very upset right now." Such acknowledgment may bring down the conversation's temperature, allowing effective communication to occur.

When hearing angry words allow the Zen mind to adjust the picture. Calmly search for the true message behind the words. Clarify the points being expressed, but try to listen more than talk. Such mindful handling of tough situations builds strong salesperson/manager relationships.

Words from the Wise
"To avoid criticism do nothing, say nothing, be nothing."
Elbert Hubbard

Younger or Less Experienced Managers

As you age as a sales professional, more of your managers will inevitably be younger than you. It's a trifling matter, actually, if your boss has fewer years on the planet—or fewer years in the industry—than you. What *is* important is their managerial effectiveness, and your ability and willingness to allow them to do their job.

The days of straight-line, age-equals-seniority employment are long gone. Even in regimented structures such as the military and the police, a young lieutenant is superior in rank to an older sergeant. In sales, such age-reversed reporting structures are common.

The Zen mind recognizes the need for superiority in rank, but not in importance. In the spirit of sameness, individuals may have different working roles, but one individual should never be considered better than another.

If it bothers you that a younger or less experienced person has become your manager, pause and consider why. Perhaps they have a unique work background that your company's executives decided was needed. Perhaps the executives wanted a radical change in your group's behavior. Knowing why, however, doesn't necessarily make it easier to swallow.

Avoid making assumptions about younger or less experienced managers. Few are out to replace older salespeople with younger ones. They hopefully realize two things: 1) talent is talent, regardless of age, and 2) there's a risk of an age discrimination lawsuit after replacing an employee solely because of their age.

Younger managers may not have the selling skills you have, but their job is not to do your job. Their job is to manage. They may be just as uncomfortable and uncertain managing you, as you are of being managed by them. Your level of experience may be worrisome to the manager, if they see themselves as unqualified to manage you. Reassuring your younger manager that you respect them is helpful.

Consider the title of a younger manager and communicate appropriately to avoid ill feelings. They may welcome suggestions from you, but if you speak in a condescending, parent-to-child manner, they will bristle. Instead of building a relationship you'll be building a barrier. Ask them if they're open to advice, then proceed conversationally, not offensively. Try to solicit their advice. The younger manager will appreciate the implied respect.

Younger managers rely on their sales staff, regardless of individual age. Use your maturity, and proactively take steps to welcome younger managers, and to create a mutually trusting and rewarding working relationship.

The Problem Boss

Few things are as emotionally draining as working for a problem manager. When your manager is constantly angry or unfair with you, try to objectively examine if their behavior is event-based or long-term. Is there a trigger? Have you changed the way you sell, or the way you communicate with your manager lately?

If it seems that you are not the cause, then schedule a meeting and communicate your feelings with the manager. "I know you're upset, and it's making me upset," is a non-judgmental statement that acknowledges their state of mind while also affirming your feelings.

If such a dialogue fails, you may be dealing with a manager who has anger, self-esteem or ego issues. These are difficult, if not impossible, for the subordinate employee to deal with. Try to understand that such managers are probably angry with most employees most of the time. It's likely not personal, even though it's hard to see someone being angry with you as not personal. They may be stuck in a behavioral mode or in a mindset in which anger, disrespect and put-downs are viewed as acceptable. Such behavior will probably not change overnight.

Words from the Wise

"It is a waste of energy to be angry with a man who behaves badly, just as it is to be angry with a car that won't go."
Bertrand Russell

Try to find out if company executives know about the manager's offensive style and emotional instability. If they don't, consider letting them know, although this entails some vocational risk. If they know about the manager's emotional issues but choose to do nothing, and if you are suffering from dealing with the anger, then consider seeking employment elsewhere. Stress is an acceptable element of sales. Abuse is not.

When a manager, customer or coworker says or does things that cause you emotional injury, it is imperative that you take time to re-center yourself and put things in perspective before continuing with your day. Discover which steam release mechanisms work best for you. A walk around the block, a cup of tea, or a few minutes sitting quietly to reflect are all good options. Talking with others to get something off your chest is also fine, unless it becomes a joint gripe session from which you emerge more stressed than you entered.

Exercise #18: List what you'd like to say (complimentary or critical) to your sales manager, but so far have not

- _____
- _____
- _____
- _____
- _____

Meditation is Kindness to Yourself

Splurging part of a commission payment on something that makes you feel good is fine, but don't forget that meditation is also kindness to yourself. (It's also free!)

As you meditate more often you will see the benefits increase. You will start to look forward to meditation as a respite from the pressures and demands of the day. It becomes *your time*. Counting breaths becomes less necessary because you will naturally fall into inner calmness and serenity.

Meditation isn't a path to a goal. It's an element of your journey that helps you experience peace, clarity, insight, personal power and wisdom. If you're open to it you may experience complete, blissful compassion for — and a complete connection with — everyone and everything.

Pay attention to how you feel before, during and after meditating. Consider writing down your observations after each meditation in a personal, secure journal. Read your words later and reflect on how meditation affects you in different ways.

From time to time, state the obvious. Consider how lucky you are to be who you are, to have what you have, to love the way you do, to be loved the way you are, and to have a level of opportunity and comfort that many around the world do not. You may find yourself realizing that many things you have taken for granted are actually amazing blessings.

Try out this affirmation meditation in a private, quiet spot. Sit comfortably. Inhale deeply, then exhale fully while saying or thinking these statements one at a time:

- Inhale. Exhale with, "I am alive."
- Inhale. Exhale with, "I am breathing."
- Inhale. Exhale with, "I am healthy."
- Inhale. Exhale with, "I have family."
- Inhale. Exhale with, "I have friends."
- Inhale. Exhale with, "I am loved."
- Inhale. Exhale with, "I am not hungry"
- Inhale. Exhale with, "I am not poor."
- Inhale. Exhale with, "I have much."
- Inhale. Exhale with, "I have much to give."

Affirmations may state the obvious, yet they are powerful tools. Besides helping you reclaim a sense of perspective, affirmations are useful in sorting out true problems from perceived problems. Find the affirmations that really resonate with you, and repeat them often. Write out or print the best ones, and affix them around your work area so you can glance at them throughout the day.

"In music, in the sea, in a flower, in a leaf, in an act of kindness...I see what people call God in all these things."

- Pablo Casals

9
ANYTIME AWARENESS

Active Meditation

Active meditation is applying the same mindful, in-the-moment focus techniques of seated meditation during selected activities. The best activities for this kind of meditation are simple, repetitive and do not involve or require the interaction of others. Complex tasks such as driving a car, presenting to customers, meeting with coworkers, and completing sales forecasts do not lend themselves to active meditation.

Zen monasteries encourage monks to actively meditate while performing tasks such as washing dishes, gardening, and eating. In monastic life, most of these tasks are done without conversing with others, even though others may be present.

The following solo activities may be combined with active meditation to promote a healthy mind and body:

- Yoga
- Stretching
- Walking or running
- Using a treadmill, StairMaster or rowing machine
- Lifting weights (use caution when lifting anything heavier than light weights)
- Swimming
- In-line skating.

Professional long distance runners have reported, toward the last miles of a marathon, a feeling of intense, in-the-moment connection and passion that brings tears to their eyes. The physical and mental strain they have endured in the race melt away, leaving a great clarity of mind. Some runners describe their feelings as the ultimate form of meditation, in which elevated states of consciousness, perhaps even glimpses of enlightenment, are experienced.

Active meditation has several steps:

1) Be completely aware of your body—hands, feet, arms, legs—as part of the task you are performing.
2) Establish a close physical connection with the tools you are using, and with the things you are touching:
   - dishrag and dishes
   - glove and garden rake
   - dumbbell
   - shoes or skates
   - surface of the road or treadmill.
3) Find a rhythm or timing for the task you are performing:
   - count or move to your breaths (similar to seated meditation)
   - count or feel the beat of your steps
   - count repetitions
4) Feel distractions and other thoughts disappear, replaced by total confidence and relaxation.

It is perfectly fine to stop sometimes and collect your breath, take a look around, and see others around you. Try to avoid chatting with others, however, until you are finished with your activity. Talking highlights non-meditative thought, which is counterproductive to active meditation.

Some become so enmeshed in their workout-meditations, so in-the-moment, that they have to set an audible timer alert to remind them when to stop their activity, or when to switch to another one. Now that's immersion!

The objective is to see yourself in a beautiful, efficient and sometimes effortless movement without needless intervention from the mind. If you don't experience this effect right away, don't worry about it. Just keep enjoying your activity.

Use active meditation to turn previously mundane tasks such as dish washing and gardening into wonderful opportunities for relaxation and self-improvement.

Exercise #19: List the ways you calm down your mind

- _____
- _____
- _____
- _____
- _____

Enlightenment

Zen is thought by some to be a lifelong, monastic quest for enlightenment. This view is likely drawn from images of robe-wearing Zen Buddhist monks with shaved heads living an ascetic lifestyle. Zen's roots are in Zen Buddhism, but the roots also extend to Taoism and schools of rational thinking such as transcendentalism and psychotherapy.

An *outcome* of Zen practice may be enlightenment, but Zen's emphasis is on the in-the-moment awareness, the compassionate connection and the practical enjoyment of everyday living. Regarding enlightenment, Zen teaches that:

1) You were born enlightened.
2) You are still enlightened.
3) Your natural enlightenment may simply be hidden underneath a lifetime layer of distraction, stress, worry, comparison, desire, wanting and suffering.

> ### *Lessons from a Zen Sage*
> "Enlightenment (also known as full awakeness) is a natural, ordinary state that wants to emerge. We can block this emergence with the ego, but when the dam begins to break, the clear cool refreshing waters of awareness will begin to flow...perhaps starting with just a trickle."
> Pema *Chödrön*

Enlightenment has different meanings to different people. Some definitions of enlightenment are:

- Sensing the connection and sameness between you and everyone and everything else
- Seeing the perfection in everything, without requiring your help to make it perfect
- Letting go of the ego and everything else that rigidly defines who you are
- Experiencing the *Seventh Center of Consciousness* (or *Seventh Chakra*).

If you find yourself wanting enlightenment, you may be missing the point. The word *wanting* means being without, as in, "He was hungry, but there was no food, so he went wanting." Wanting anything affirms your lack of it.

You were born enlightened, and the trick is to re-discover the enlightenment that has always been part of you. Zen teaches that a clear mind is needed to see your connection with yourself, and with the entire universe. Experiencing this connection is experiencing enlightenment. You'll know it when it happens. It's as simple as that.

In Zen the *Bodhisattva Ideal* says that one who is enlightened is constantly devoted to helping others attain enlightenment. Characteristics of the Bodhisattva Ideal are defined in the *Six Perfections*, which are:

1) Generosity
2) Discipline
3) Patience
4) Energy
5) Meditation
6) Wisdom

Lessons from a Zen Sage

"Enlightenment, for a wave in the ocean, is the moment the wave realizes it is water."
Thich Nhat Hanh

The Simple Rewards of Meditation

People often want something to *happen* during meditation. If you need something to happen, something to *do* while meditating, then pay attention to your breathing and your thoughts. Count your breaths, feel the warmth of your exhalations, watch your belly rise and fall, and marvel at the way your thoughts pop up from nowhere.

Meditation is focused relaxation — including relaxation of the brain — that enables centeredness. When in a calm, centered place, you can see your true nature.

When experiencing life on a deeper level, you realize that everyone looks up to the same sky. The only difference is in what one chooses to see there.

The results of meditation are sometimes huge and sometimes no big deal. Both are perfect outcomes, with their own unique opportunities for learning. If you become stuck in a meditational rut, change the scene. Do it in another place, at another time. If you've tried it with an empty stomach, try it after a meal. Not working well while sitting cross-legged? Try it sitting on the edge of a chair.

Seek small changes, small adjustments, through meditation. You may one day have an epiphany, a major movement in your psyche. If so, congratulations. If not, you're making progress gradually, which is just as good.

As you progress through personal meditation, ask yourself, from time to time, "What is important to me?" "What do I value?" Are there things in life that you have held onto so tightly that your grasp is growing weary and weak? What happens if you release your grip on some of these things? Are you now different? Are you able to laugh — or at least smile — at some of the things you consider must-haves? It's healthy to periodically question and update your list of desires.

What if you held onto no beliefs, yet were open to everything, everyone, and all experiences, without judgment? Few, if any, absolute answers exist, but there will always be questions. The questions asked define the person doing the asking. Finding your unique questions will take a lifetime, but what an *alive* lifetime it will be.

Exercise #20: List the best elements of your spiritual or personal self that you use everyday in sales

- _____
- _____
- _____
- _____
- _____

Tell Yourself Why You Work

How do you view selling as a profession? Are you sometimes embarrassed by the label *salesperson*? Are you proud of it? A little of both? Do you see the honor in what you do?

How do you describe to others what you do? Perhaps you see yourself not as a salesperson but as an expert in your industry. For example, advertising sales representatives for newspapers may see themselves as, "…in media," as opposed to, "…in sales."

Something to Consider

Salespeople who see themselves primarily as *educators of trends and providers of technological advancements* are received more warmly by customers than salespeople who see themselves as merely somebody who sells products.

What do you verbally or non-verbally say to yourself in the morning as you prepare for work? If it's something like, "I have to try to sell things today?" remember that 'have to' denotes a chore, a tedium to be avoided if possible, or at least an activity that is not your first choice.

Why are you working? What are you working for? Often, money is a prime motivator, but you still have plenty of free choice regarding which company, which industry, which location, and with whom you work. Perhaps you're in the perfect position, where you are. Or perhaps the grass truly is greener elsewhere. Think about it first, then write down your personal why-I-work statement. This statement will ideally mesh with the values you've written down earlier. Here's an example of a *why-I-work statement*:

"I work as a salesperson for Heimlich Industries because it provides me with a good income, an expert rating in the field of mechanical actuators, a chance to move into management, and countless opportunities to work on myself and become a better spouse and parent."

Exercise #21: Write down your personal why-I-work statement

_____

_____

_____

_____

_____

Such a statement becomes a buoyant pre-work affirmation. Satisfaction and happiness result when your daily actions have deep, personal meaning. Everything you do becomes a reflection of your true values. Everything that happens to you—including the bad things—is a necessary step in your journey and your development of awareness.

Over time, reexamine, refine and rewrite your why-I-work statement.

It's possible to work without such a statement. Many do. Work, however, is a remarkable way to experience happiness, so why not use it as a tool for personal growth? With your Zen mind, aim for the *middle way* when approaching work—somewhere between a dreadful "I hate my job" and a maniacal "Woo-hoo! I get to sell today!" Develop an affinity for living between extremes, yet always see work as a teacher offering valuable lessons.

If seen as a negative experience, work becomes a self-fulfilling prophecy in which:

× Each task is viewed a drudging chore that must be done then checked off.
× The clock ticks slowly toward daily quitting time.
× The calendar moves slowly toward the weekend.
× Prospects, customers, coworkers and managers are viewed as tolerated irritants.
× Your job is simply a way to pay the bills.

Such an outlook provides little opportunity for fulfillment and development of awareness. Sales is your occupation, not your life or your identity, yet it's what you have chosen to do for many hours each day, many days each year. Most people spend more awake-hours at work than with their spouse or partner. The choice *not* to enjoy the work you've chosen will inevitably lead you to resentfully ask, at some point in the future, "Why did I waste those years?"

You are entitled to a positive outlook. All you have to do is choose it.

Exercise #22: List when you've felt the most fulfilled and happy as a salesperson

- _____
- _____
- _____
- _____
- _____

Embrace Failure and Examine Fear

Most failures have at least a modicum of wisdom that can be translated into a lesson. Some lessons are profound. Losing a sale stings, sometimes badly. Gathering wisdom from a loss requires first acknowledging, then treating, the wound. Later, when the sting has worn off a bit, consider how to avoid similar occurrences in the future.

Lessons from a Zen Sage

"Not getting what you want is sometimes a wonderful stroke of luck."
  The Dalai Lama

No one grows and learns without failure. From toddlers who fall down repeatedly until they learn to walk across the living room, to CEOs who rebuild their company's image and operation after a devastating bankruptcy, the lessons that failure brings are necessary steps to growth.

Few embrace and encourage failure, yet the opposite position—avoiding any chance of failure by playing it safe—all but ensures that progress won't happen. You have two choices after suffering a failure as a salesperson:

1) React with resentment and fear of it happening again, or
2) React with an enhanced degree of awareness, and a willingness to try it again, this time with additional knowledge and skill.

Fear of failure has an odd cousin, fear of success. Some salespeople are subconsciously afraid of being successful. Perhaps they:

- Have observed successful salespeople who don't match their idea of a *nice person*
- Have seen the negative aspects of earning lots of money
- Are unsure how successful people are *supposed* to act around coworkers, management, family and friends
- Don't trust themselves enough to be successful.

The unfortunate consequence of fear of success is *lack* of success. You avoid what you fear. Fear of success keeps unproductive behavior going strong. Meditation and introspection of your true values helps identify fear of failure, and fear of success.

Exercise #23: List the lessons you've learned from significant sales losses in your career

- _____
- _____
- _____
- _____
- _____

Mend What's Not Working

Failure in selling is either short- or long-term. Further analysis breaks down short- and long-term sales failure as either externally- or internally-caused.

Spend only a brief time examining short-term failures, such as losing an individual sale to a customer. Uncover the reasons for the loss by asking the customer, "What could I, and my company, have done differently?" Later, ask yourself, "What could I have done differently?" The reward for humbly asking such questions—and closely listening to the answers—is a quick lesson in self-awareness and self-improvement.

Long term failure in sales requires intense evaluation. After awhile, bad luck exits the picture as a possible cause. External reasons for long-term sales failure likely point to a poor match between salesperson qualifications and experience in a particular industry, geography or customer level. A freshly minted college graduate calling on seasoned high-level executives is an obvious example of the latter.

Are you properly engaging all available company resources—especially your sales manager—as you sell? Let your manager know what you're working on, how you're doing it and the trade-offs and risks involved. Be open to their guidance. Sales losses that occur under such disclosure become company losses, not just personal losses.

Internal reasons for long term sales failure are harder to peg. If the culprit is poor sales habits, decide that you are committed to improving time management and decision making skills.

Poor prospect selection is a great contributor to failure in sales. Spending valuable time selling to those who have little chance of—or interest in—buying, takes time away from selling to better-qualified prospects. Knowing when to walk away from a customer is the hallmark of a savvy rep. Chasing a big name customer may be alluring, but if your products aren't a good fit for practical or political reasons, refocusing on other, perhaps smaller, opportunities makes more sense.

Internal reasons for long term sales failure caused by lifestyle and behavioral issues are the most difficult to deal with. These include:

- Excess substance use: alcohol, coffee, drugs or food

- Compelling behaviors that mix pleasure with harm: gambling, spending or sex

- Pain avoidance: lying, avoiding commitments or procrastinating.

The first two reasons may require the affected salesperson to seek professional assistance and counseling. The third reason, pain avoidance through lying, avoiding commitments, and procrastinating, may also indicate professional counseling, but an initial self-examination of the underlying causes couldn't hurt.

Consider what you gain and lose from such behavior. The gain from pain avoidance is immediate and short-term, but that is quickly overshadowed by the loss. Losses from pain avoidance escalate from losing a trusting relationship with your manager, to losing sales and commission payments, to losing your job...all as a result of lies, missed commitments or procrastination. Sometimes just visualizing the downsides to such behavior is enough to induce a turnaround in behavior.

The final reason for long-term, internal failure is a lack of compatibility between the salesperson's unique personality and the profession of selling in general. If you hate competitive situations, if you are externally (not internally) motivated, if you dislike—or have trouble—talking with others, then sales is likely a poor career choice. A different occupation may allow you to thrive, and to be much happier.

10
ADVICE ON SUCCESSFUL, MINDFUL SELLING

Accept—Then Forget—Your Quota

Salespeople live and (hopefully figuratively) die by the quota. Few salespeople know, at the beginning of their quarterly or monthly sales cycle, where each dollar of their revenue will come from. Yet consistently successful salespeople seem to know that they will reach their quota, without being able to elucidate exactly how. You could say they have a certain *Zen* about it.

Successful salespeople focus on standard selling metrics. They know that if they keep finding new prospects to add to their pipeline, keep focused on closing current customers, and keep open to assistance from all sources, their quota will somehow be achieved.

Quotas are necessary to measure product, marketing and salesforce effectiveness, and also to manage and report revenue growth. Individual quota assignments are derived by taking the company's overall revenue target and dividing it by the number of sales team areas. Some sales teams have larger quotas than others because of varying market potential. Each team manager then assigns a portion of their quota to individual team members. Quota revenue must be collected by a certain date. Salespeople often sign an agreement—a commitment—that they will find a way to bring in their assigned revenue.

A leap of faith is required by each salesperson assigned a quota. "Somehow, I will sell that much product," is a commitment to yourself as well as to the company. Quotas facilitate stress, and performing under stress produces unpredictable results.

Some deals will close, some will be lost. Some *bluebirds* will pop up out of nowhere to create unexpected revenue, and some deals that seemed a sure thing will be lost at the eleventh hour.

A salesperson with a track record has an advantage over newer reps in the area of historical averaging and future estimation. Over time they can determine the average percentage of pipeline revenue that becomes actual revenue. That figure may be used to reduce quota stress by simply building up the pipeline until the end result appears achievable.

For example, if the sales cycles in which you historically met quota began with forty pipeline opportunities, averaging $35,000 each, then future cycles with an equivalent number and dollar value are likely to produce similar results. This assumes that additional pipeline opportunities are added throughout all cycles.

Many salespeople live in fear of the quota. Fear is healthy only when it protects you from harm, otherwise it's useless and often harmful. Fear-based selling becomes desperation-based selling if, beyond the mid-point of the quota's time window, sufficient revenue isn't coming in. Fear causes salespeople to close down, to self-protect, to run and hide. Savvy customers have a knack for smelling fear on salespeople. They hear it in the tone of voice. Customers take advantage by demanding pricing and other concessions that ordinarily wouldn't be given away. You can't blame them. You'd do the same thing in their shoes.

One of the worst side effects of quotas is pricing concessions made toward the end of the sales cycle, ostensibly, "...to create some much-needed revenue." Quota-induced price-cutting affects the delicate financial balance between minimum profit margins and minimum revenue reporting. Such price cuts will haunt salespeople and management for months after the sale. Customer expectations are forever altered by end-of-cycle pricing reductions. Smart customers learn a new pressure point. They will use that pressure point in the future by delaying purchases until the salesperson relents. *Keep pricing concessions to a minimum.*

See your quota as neither positive nor negative, simply a measurement tool used by management. Stressing out about your quota is counterproductive. Receive your quota, acknowledge it, then forget about it (New York accent optional). Focus your energy on the techniques presented in *ZenWise Selling*. The quota will take care of itself.

Exercise #24: List the advice you'd give to a person starting their first job in sales

- _____
- _____
- _____
- _____
- _____

Seek Shades of Gray

The world is often seen in black and white. It makes descriptions simple...something is either good or bad, right or wrong. The downside is that using stereotypical generalizations to describe yourself, customers, coworkers, management, occupations, religions and ethnicities limits your ability to see things as they really are. Black and white creates separation where none should exist.

Stereotyping is often based in fear, lack of knowledge or limited experience. Examples are:

- "I'd never hire a _____."
- "All _____ are _____."
- "You can't trust _____."

Such single-minded assertions actually define the speaker more clearly that the object. Once expressed to family, friends and coworkers, stereotypical statements are difficult, if not impossible, to live down.

A valid argument is that experience is the best teacher. Old adages such as, "Once bitten, twice shy," exist for a reason. After a couple of poor experiences involving similar *types* of customers, a salesperson's temptation may be to group all such customers into the same not-worth-the-effort bucket. From a statistical viewpoint, however, a sample size of "a couple" is too small to be meaningful. The next effort may have been positive and profitable. Self-imposed restrictions can be costly.

Gray is the combination of black and white, including both, excluding neither. When black and white labels are removed, there may be an initial sense of discomfort. "What do I *call* it?" "How do I *describe* it?" Given time, the discomfort wears off, leaving a soothing commonality...a grayness.

Gray comes in infinite shades, similar to the infinite circumstances that make up everyone and everything. Seeking shades of gray entails compromise. Compromise does not require *giving up* of one's true nature. Compromise is openness to seeing the world though the eyes of another, and consideration of what could result from the merger of different viewpoints.

Zen's middle way through life is colored gray, not black or white. Compassion and flexibility play large parts in Zen philosophy, as do associated attributes including wisdom, patience and humor. Through grayness one truly connects with other human beings by:

- Seeing them through eyes that are attuned to *shared* experiences and emotions
- Feeling them with a heart that is sympathetic to their dilemmas
- Touching them with a genuine desire for their well-being.

In philosophy, as in everyday life, one's own beliefs are often considered more worthy than those of others. Yet most philosophies and approaches have at least some merit. This is not to say that completely switching beliefs is wise either. Westerners who denounce their region's philosophies as rubbish and who adopt Eastern thought *exclusively* are just as black and white as Easterners who completely give up their heritage in favor of Western culture.

Lessons from a Zen Sage

"Where there is beauty, there is ugliness. When something is right, something else is wrong. Knowledge and ignorance depend on each other. Delusion and enlightenment condition each other. It has been like this since the beginning. How could it be otherwise now? Wanting to throw out one and hold on to the other makes for a ridiculous comedy. You must still deal with everything, ever changing, even when you say it's all wonderful."
Zen Master Ryokan (died 1831), known for his kindness and poetry

---

Grayness in selling means minimizing assumptions and taking responsibility for the outcome of each transaction and each customer relationship, regardless of your prior luck in similar circumstances.

Assumptions in sales are only beneficial when dealing with circumstances beyond your control. Base promises you make to a customer on an assumption of the *worst case scenario*. Recall a long delay you've encountered with your company's shipping department, and factor that delay into your estimate to your customer regarding the not-later-than ship date for the product they purchased. Hoping for—and even worse, promising—the *best* possible outcome in such circumstances may lead to customer disappointment and frustration.

Smile, Compliment and Thank

The middle path of grayness is made even sweeter when you infuse everyday life with humor and a smile. Not insincere smiles, or I'm-hurting-but-don't-want-to-admit-it smiles, but smiles that appeal to—and disarm—those on the receiving end. Watch what happens when you smile at a harried checkout clerk at the grocery store. You brighten a moment for them, and you may receive a great smile in return. Some people seldom smile. Keep offering them yours. You have an endless supply.

Kindness and friendliness are corollaries to smiling. Pepper sentences with "please" and "thank you." Offer to bring coffee or water to coworkers and customers. Popping out for a noontime sandwich? Survey the office for others who could use a bite if they're working through lunch.

Make a nice comment about a coworker's new jacket, or compliment them in some other way. Everyone likes to hear that they've done something well. Write thank you notes and cards for the smallest of reasons. Make thank you phone calls. Do all of this without the expectation of reciprocity.

Unselfish acts feel good, and they reflect positively on you. It may be a cumulative, long-term transformation, but over time you'll notice those around you expressing more kindness to each other.

Confront Gently

Confrontation, for salespeople, is part of doing business. Confrontation itself does not conflict with the principles of Zen. Disagreements may be resolved harshly or gently, it's your choice. When someone initiates a difficult subject in an angry tone, the responding party often becomes angry too. Yet the reverse is also true. Gentle yet firm language is powerfully effective, and it keeps emotions under control.

Gentle confrontation enables flexibility on both sides. Differing viewpoints are brought to light, illuminating what wasn't known or understood before. Another's viewpoints are difficult to see when presented in anger or frustration. Treading lightly promotes mutual understanding and lessens hurt feelings.

Avoid Complainers

Avoid coworkers who complain too much. Regularly listening to their remarks may lead to their cynicism and anger being rubbed off onto you. Unfortunately, avoidance may be difficult if the complainer is influential in the organization.

A coworker who constantly complains may have valid issues, they may see complaining as a way of uniting others around their cause, or they may simply enjoy complaining. Either way, little good comes from spending more than a few minutes discussing their gripe. If they have a valid point, it's up to them to stop talking about it and start taking action.

Few easy ways exist to deal with a coworker who speaks badly about the company, coworkers or management. Disassociation from the person may be impossible, inappropriate or rude. You can try validating their position ("I see how you can feel that way") and offering alternate viewpoints that may shed some positive light on their issue. If that doesn't help, try to find ways to spend less time with that person, or gently but firmly inform them that you have to return to work.

Luckily, cheerfulness is more contagious than cynicism. Remain as centered, enthusiastic and confident in your work as possible. Others may see and adopt your positive attitude and behavior.

Manage Your Workload

Think carefully before taking on new named accounts, a bigger territory, accelerated prospecting, or more deadline-measurable action items. It's easy to add on more than you can handle. A *can-do* attitude is fantastic, but broken promises, missed commitments and a bottomless in-basket are not.

Ensure you are ready, willing and qualified to handle new tasks. It's often difficult or impossible to just say no to an assigned task. If given a new task by your manager, ask enough questions about what's expected—the outcome, the due date, others involved in the task—until you are confident in your ability to do the job.

If you feel uncertain about your ability to complete the task, say so as soon as possible. Waiting until the task is due before announcing, "Sorry, I didn't understand," engenders little sympathy.

Manage Your Time

Richard Carlson, in his book *Don't Sweat the Small Stuff at Work*, has a great idea. Create a small sign, he writes, saying, "Am I Making the Absolute Best of This Moment?" and display it where you work.[15] Glancing at the sign from time to time will refocus your attention on what's important.

When you receive a hot lead or a phone number of a prospect to call, call it immediately, if you're prepared. Delay increases the risk of forgetting to call. For salespeople prone to procrastination, calling right away means the task is complete, and not added to an already tall pile of action items.

Use a paper log or a computer system to prioritize daily tasks using the familiar *A/B/C* system. *A* tasks *must* be done. *B* tasks *should* be done, but only after the *A*s. *C* tasks may slip a day or two if necessary. Allocate enough time—including time for breaks and meals—to complete each task.

Once you start a task, don't stop until it's completed. An hour working in a focused, non-distracted, uninterrupted mode produces the same or better results as two or more hours that are peppered with distracted thoughts and attention-grabbing interruptions.

Exercise #25: List the sales tasks you tend to procrastinate about

- _____
- _____
- _____
- _____
- _____

Manage Your Personal Budget

Salespeople are rewarded, sometimes handsomely, for their efforts. Money is a great reward, but a poor end in itself. Money provides opportunities and options, but money has downsides too. If you develop an opulent lifestyle that assumes a constant, high-level of income, stress comes roaring in if that income drops.

Worth a Smile

"Tell me that you want those kinds of things that money just can't buy. For I don't care too much for money. Money can't buy me love."
Lennon & McCartney

Live somewhat below your means, not barely within them. Save or invest the difference. Such a buffer zone may someday come in handy. The more money you have, the more you should donate to worthy, charitable causes that you feel strongly about. Good causes are plentiful. In the three seconds it takes to read this sentence, twenty-one children died from hunger, somewhere on the planet.

Some managers encourage their sales staff with this advice: "Buy the most expensive car out there. You'll look great driving it. Besides, I like my salespeople to sweat a little about money. That way you'll work harder and sell more. Ha! Ha!" This is bad advice.

A stressed-out salesperson is not effective. Having some money left over at the end of the month will reduce stress and allow you to focus your energies positively and creatively. Having a calm mind and a shiny new Honda Accord in the driveway is better than having a fearful mind and a shiny new BMW 7-series. Consider Zen's *middle way* when selecting a vehicle. Strike a balance between practicality and opulence. The best car for a traveling sales rep who often transports customers is a clean, comfortable, efficient, new-ish, four-door sedan that reflects well on the owner. A gas-guzzling, *urban assault vehicle* may convey the wrong image about both the salesperson and their company to the customer.

Spending your income intelligently extends to houses and lifestyles. It's easy to cut back on dining out when sales are lean, but not so easy to cut back on the mortgage or rent payment. Spending less each month doesn't have to mean a lowered standard of living. Managing your personal budget well enables you to save money for relaxing cruises, vacations, tuition, retirement, and a financial safety net.

CFOs ensure that company income exceeds expenditures. Why run your personal budget any differently? You'll enjoy your job more when you see it as not just a means to pay for goods, but also as a reflection of who you are and what you value.

Reward Yourself

When you win a big deal, celebrate! You deserve it. Take a loved one out for a nice dinner. Buy something that makes you feel good, but that doesn't bankrupt you. Bask in the warm glow of success. Sales is a *what-have-you-done-for-me-lately?* profession, and victory is soon forgotten. Treat yourself well consistently, but do so especially after you've accomplished something of value.

Salespeople around you will congratulate your win, but deep inside they may see added pressure for their own wins to materialize. They may feel jealous or even threatened. Respect their emotions. You've been there too. Try to avoid bragging, especially in front of coworkers. Practice humility.

Rewarding yourself isn't just for closing deals. Brief, restorative periods during the day are excellent *mini-rewards*. Without breaks in your work routine you will become less focused, and unfocused minds wander. When you notice this happening, consider the wandering to be signal for a brief break. Scheduling breaks at a particular time is fine for some, but it's best to reward yourself with a time-out when the need arises.

Physical stretching, even while sitting at your desk, is another personal reward. Yoga is wonderful if you've taken a class and you have the physical space and privacy in your office. Alternatively, take a refreshing walk around the block. Sometimes just a walk around the office corridors will do the trick.

Try not to use your personal break time as merely chit-chat time with coworkers. Your break time may not necessarily be theirs. Physical, emotional and spiritual renewal is best done as a solo activity...at least while at work.

Be Passionate

Salespeople who are passionate about their customers and their products have an advantage over those who lack passion. Display your passion in levels that match the circumstances. Too much passion for a particular situation will hinder the ability to clearly listen and speak.

It's a compliment to describe a salesperson as passionate about winning. A more refined compliment is to describe their enthusiastic passion to do the best possible work for the customer. Passion for winning may entail winning at any cost. Passion for the customer's satisfaction focuses effort on win-win objectives.

Throwing yourself into work is terrific, but passion is not a constant flame. Those who are regularly passionate sometimes feel the flame flicker and burn out. Don't be too quick to re-light. Recognizing, honoring, and analyzing the *loss* of passion is just as important as utilizing the passion when it appears.

When passion results in a sales victory, be happy. Thank others who were instrumental in helping the sale close, and consider rewarding them with a lunch, a dinner or a drink...some person-to-person way of expressing your appreciation. When another wins, be aware of feelings of envy and jealousy. Resentment of another's success indicates a sense of incompleteness and dissatisfaction with yourself.

When passion results in a sales loss, be sad. Consider taking some time to just breathe and meditate. You're the same good person you were before the loss. Your passion will re-ignite and lead you away from the loss, and toward the next challenge. When another loses a sale, send sympathetic understanding their way. Avoid the temptation to rationalize or minimize their loss.

Don't judge the passion of others. When you are down, it's easy to see another's exuberance as manic nonsense. If possible, try to draw from their happiness and elation. Use their emotional fuel to spark your stalled out engine. Passion can be catching.

Make Slow, Easy Changes In Your Selling Style

The beautiful thing about sales—and about life—is that you are free to redefine yourself at any time. Self-change isn't always smooth, however. It may be downright traumatic. At the least, major change brings on a justifiable fear of what will happen next. At the extreme, change will alienate those around you. "What's got into that person?" they may say.

Changes in selling behavior are best implemented in stages...not all at once. Managers and peers, seeing your changes in selling style and habits, will take notice. They may or may not say something. If they say something it may be either complimentary or critical.

According to researcher Dr. Stephen Fried, behavior changed *slowly* generally continues *longer* than behavior changed rapidly. If things change too quickly, unforeseen setbacks may dampen a high-spirited, all-or-nothing attitude. Also, slowness makes it possible to enjoy and savor each element of the change.

> ## Lessons from a Zen Sage
> (This Zen-like parable is told from a Western perspective.) The bush pilot asked the American Indian how long it took him to reach his trapping cabin by canoe. *"Four days,"* was the Indian's reply. The pilot chuckled and told the Indian it would take only an hour by pontoon plane. *"Why?"* remarked the Indian.

Change is a great time for introspection. If a new manager takes over, if you change jobs within the same company, or if you move to a different company, consider the change an opportunity to examine and redefine aspects of your selling style. A new boss, a new staff, new coworkers—all these things allow you to revisit how you act and interact.

Talk to Yourself with a Selling Journal

Keep a selling journal to document the changes in your selling style, and to record your feelings about it. This is psychologically sound *self-talk*. When a salesperson focuses on internal change, cognitive benefits appear too. In other words, you become smarter as you work on your inner self.

> ## Words from the Wise
> *"The individual in a state of self-awareness, more often than not, actually talks to himself or herself and uses words to describe his or her personal characteristics, behaviors, emotions, sensations, motivations, and so on. Also, evidence suggests that highly self-conscious persons, compared with low self-conscious individuals, extensively talk to themselves about themselves."*
> Alain Morin, Ph.D.[16]

Buy a good quality, blank notebook. Decide where you'll keep it...ideally in a place easy for you to access, yet difficult for others to find. Inside, jot down in informal prose your thoughts and feelings about specific selling activities. Write in your journal soon after events occur. Add general musings on sales, such as what it means to you, and what you want from it in the future.

Although it's possible to maintain a sales journal as a word processing file on a computer, putting pen to paper seems to captures the honest, unalterable truth of your feelings. In a computer file it's easy to delete a paragraph that you later decide is too revealing or sensitive. On paper the medium is more permanent—*warts and all*—for later reflection and self-learning.

The benefits of maintaining a sales journal include:

- Writing down your feelings is a form of meditation, thereby stimulating personal growth.
- Your inner self is exposed, thus setting the stage for introspection.
- Difficult sales events are noted as *closed* when written down. The past is the past. Writing is a release.
- Past feelings about events can be reviewed in the future, for insight into your progress and development.
- Journaling is the lowest cost counseling available. Your words are your feedback—honest and without judgment.
- You see trends in your career, for cause/effect analysis.
- You see the humor in sales situations.
- You see the spirituality in sales situations.
- You gather material from which you may teach others from your experience.

If you are unsure what to write about in a selling journal, consider expanding upon the list exercises in this book. Here are some additional starter topics for a selling journal. Expand the list below to include what's really important to you:

- Calling and speaking with prospects
- Meeting with, and presenting to, customers

- Your industry, and the products you sell
- Rejection by a prospect, and losing a sale to a competitor
- Winning a key sale despite the odds
- Your selling habits
- Your most frustrating customers
- Your best customers
- Your company and your manager
- Your evolving definition of success in sales.

When you start a new selling journal there won't be much writing to look back and reflect upon, until some time goes by. While your journal grows, consider digging up old proposals, emails and memos you've written in the past. This is just as edifying as reviewing a fully-stocked journal. How has your tone, your voice and your selling style evolved over the last few years? You may be amazed to recall what you wrote.

A 20-Step Recipe for a Good Day of Selling

1) Sleep well the night before.
2) Wake up slowly. Don't immediately jump out of bed in the morning. Look around the room. What do you see? What do you hear? Did you dream? Do you recall your dream? Breathe deeply as you stand up beside the bed. Say to yourself, "Wow! I'm alive!"
3) Spend a few minutes by yourself before breakfast. Meditate, or simply reflect quietly.
4) Eat a healthy breakfast. You need energy to face the day.
5) Leave early for work. Allowing enough time for possible traffic jams means you'll often arrive earlier and less stressed. Use the extra time in your office to meditate, relax, sip coffee, and plan your day.
6) Listen to low-volume music at work. Classical is soothing, but any style is fine. Some studies have shown that listening to Bach helps with relaxation and meditation, while Mozart helps with breathing and brain function.

7) Add personal items to your desk. A photo of those you love should stand out. Add affirmations, motivations and tasteful humor. Your inspirational messages may spur others seeing them to adopt yours, or to create their own.

8) Keep a selling journal.

9) Smile at others at work.

10) Practice time management and office organization skills.

11) Complete each task you start. Minimize interruptions until the task is complete.

12) Honor your emotions. When you win a deal, or make progress with a customer, celebrate! When you lose a deal or suffer a setback with a customer, acknowledge the sadness, re-center yourself — consider a quick meditation break — then jump back on the horse that threw you.

13) Practice and rehearse good presentation skills. Communicate verbally and non-verbally to the best of your ability. Represent yourself and your company well.

14) Act in accordance with your values.

15) If you are stuck in the same office all day, be sure to take frequent stretch breaks. Try to leave the office for some fresh air during lunch. A brisk walk is even better.

16) Avoid coworkers who complain, gossip or chit-chat too much.

17) Don't stay late at work on a regular basis. Before leaving the office, relax quietly in your chair and think about the day. How was it? Productive? Fulfilling? Jot a note to yourself about tasks that must be accomplished first thing the next day, and leave it on your desk.

18) When you leave the office, leave it completely. Stress and worry about work has no place at home. Whenever possible, don't take your office work home with you.

19) If you run your business from home, work in a work-only area. Stay focused by minimizing non-work interruptions. Home-office workers must also take regular breaks away from the computer and the telephone.

20) Keep your body—the most incredible instrument you'll ever own—in tip top *mechanical condition*. Eat well, exercise, and don't be afraid to have fun with your body. Envision your body as a beautiful, classic show-car manufactured in the year you were born. Treat your "car" with the utmost in loving care. Perform regular, preventative maintenance. It'll reciprocate the favor with years of reliable service.

Exercise #26: List the first things you always do to begin each workday

- _____
- _____
- _____
- _____
- _____

Sell Comfortably

If you often sell while sitting behind a desk or a computer monitor, remember that discomfort while sitting will hamper your ability to sell in-the-moment. Four recommendations when sitting at a desk and operating a computer are:

1) Sit in a comfortable chair

   If your company won't provide a supportive chair, consider buying one yourself. (Label it as your personal property.) If your chair has no—or poor—lumbar support, use a lumbar pillow. Sitting straight reduces back strain.

2) View an easy-on-the-eyes computer display.

   LCD (liquid crystal diode) flat panel display screens have no electrons shooting toward you as do CRT (cathode ray tube) monitors. They also use less electricity. (Their downside:

reduced color accuracy.) Again, if the company won't supply it, buy it yourself and consider it an investment in your health and comfort.

3) Align your wrist and arms to prevent repetitive stress injury from using the keyboard and mouse.

   Keyboards should slide out from below your desk. Using a laptop computer atop a desk — with no external keyboard — for extended periods of time is asking for pain.

4) Stand-up, move around and stretch regularly.

Avoid these five contributors to headaches, strain and pain while working behind a desk and a computer:

1) Insufficient lighting, or lighting that produces glare.

   Consider installing *natural spectrum* fluorescent and incandescent light bulbs.

2) Badly organized working tools, such as frequently used items — telephone, pens, paper, paper clips, staplers — placed more than a short reach away.

   Use a document holder to position price lists and prospect calling lists so that they face you at the same angle as your computer monitor.

3) Disorganized paperwork and general clutter preventing ready access to needed files and other items.

4) Slumping body posture that creates a downward spiral of discomfort and stress. Leaning backward in a chair tends to create downward-tilted neck stress.

5) Cradling a handset phone between your ear and your shoulder to simultaneously type, write or handle papers with your free hands.

Instead of risking offending customers by using a speaker-phone, use a hands-free headset if you need to use your hands while speaking on the phone.

If you share a computer station with other workers, take the time to adjust chair height, keyboard placement and computer viewing angles to suit you before beginning your work. Keep objects away from the space under your desk, to give your legs room to move around.

When you feel your body is in discomfort, listen to its message and adjust accordingly. Move around and stretch. Even a brief in-the-chair stretch is helpful. Simply raise your arms and flex your joints. Throughout the day remember to breathe with deep, invigorating, mind-clearing breaths.

Design Your Office for Creative Thinking

Whether or not you believe in all of its precepts, *Feng Shui* (pronounced "fung-shway") has much good advice to offer regarding the practical and aesthetic layout and furnishing of home and office. Feng means wind, and Shui means water. As in many Eastern practices, it embraces harmony with nature and the native environment. Technically described as the ancient study of physical environments, the object of Feng Shui is to create the essence of a gentle wind and smooth water, signifying good health and good harvest, all in perfect balance. This is the balance between Yin and Yang.

Feng Shui-trained architects in the East design skyscrapers for optimal energy flow. Front doors must face a certain direction, and the grounds must be free from *poison arrows* and other design flaws that may affect the success and well-being of the building's occupants.

Although Western interest with Feng Shui peaked and then leveled off in the late 1990s, the amount of time salespeople spend in their offices and cubicles justifies examining more comfortable designs. Some common sense recommendations for office design that focus on the physical and emotional needs of the worker include:

- Keep sales offices simply decorated.
- Keep desktops tidy and free from clutter.
- Use living plants to create oxygen and add earth elements to offices.
- Try to work in an office with a window that looks out upon, and connects with, the outside world.
- Sit in comfortable chairs.
- Create a private area if possible.
- Adjust phone ringers for less-abrasive tones.

Love the Ordinary

Walking down any new pathway, such as Zen, doesn't enable you to instantly drop emotional baggage you've accumulated over a lifetime. Zen may change your perceptions and reactions, but not immediately and seldom completely. Change will be gradual, and you'll see the evidence of change in the most ordinary of ways.

Zen helps you see ordinary events, objects and people in extraordinary ways. The simple act of listening to a coworker speak about their weekend becomes mesmerizing. A hummingbird hovering outside your window awes you...even if you see the same coworker, and same hummingbird, every day.

With practice, even negative energy from others — such as an angry driver in the next lane — can elicit a deep compassion. It'll feel strange at first. Go with the feeling. Compassion — like enlightenment—has always been there, inside you, but it can easily be hidden or misplaced. Selflessly focusing on helping others is evidence of the reemergence of mindfulness.

No clap of thunder will announce the progress you've made. Calmness of mind and spirit are ordinary things. Your love of the ordinary means you are experiencing and rediscovering whom you truly are.

Final Thoughts

When you see yourself and those around you as beautifully unique, as having a peaceful enlightenment bubbling just below the surface, you experience a sense of universal connection that opens hearts and open doors. The only moment you truly have is right here, right now. May you find beauty in all things. May you experience the joy of living as you rejoice in the experience of selling.

"What lies behind us and
what lies before us are
tiny matters compared to
what lies within us."
- Ralph Waldo Emerson

APPENDIX A:
THE STORY BEHIND ZEN

Young Prince Turned Wandering Seeker

About 2,600 years ago, Siddhartha Gautama walked away from his luxurious castle home, his wife and his young child. He set off to roam the Northern Indian countryside in search of wisdom. He was 29 years old at the time. On his travels he explored various philosophies and teachings. At age 35, after six years of study and meditation, he was enlightened.

Siddhartha was the well-to-do prince of a clan in the Himalayan foothills. Growing up, young Prince Siddhartha was restricted to the castle by order of his father, the king. The king did not want Siddhartha to see the ugly world outside. By his mid-twenties Siddhartha had been trained as an expert in archery, swordsmanship and wrestling, yet he was restless. Even his marriage to a beautiful princess and the birth of his son did nothing to alleviate his discontent.

One day he left the castle walls and ventured for the first time into the village. He saw old people, sick people, and rotting corpses. On his way back to the castle he saw a poor, simple man wandering peacefully by the road. Wealth and luxury, he saw, did not guarantee happiness. Deciding that an ascetic lifestyle was better for gathering knowledge and understanding, Siddhartha left the castle forever, abandoning his family and his riches. With his sword he cut his long hair. He gave away his fine clothes in exchange for simple robes.

To reach enlightenment, Siddhartha placed himself under the tutelage of one teacher after another, learning how to discipline his mind. He and five companions practiced austerity and concentration for several years. Some days he took only water and a single grain of rice. He was disappointed that his teachers had failed to help him attain an understanding of the endless cycles of life, suffering and death he saw all around.

Seeing his severe emaciation his friends led him to a village for food and recuperation. With his strength back, the thirty-five year old Siddhartha found a Bodhi tree and sat beneath it for six days and nights, barely moving.

Suddenly he opened his eyes and realized that what he had been looking for was something that he had never lost. There was, he saw, nothing to attain, and consequently no need to struggle to attain this *nothingness.*

His reported words were: "Wonder of wonders! All sentient beings have the same [enlightened] nature, yet they are unhappy for the lack of it!" He then became known as the Buddha, translated from the Sanskrit root *budh,* meaning the awakened one.

At first he was hesitant to teach his realizations, for fear that no one would understand. Coming across his five ascetic companions again, the Buddha was soon convinced to teach them what he'd learned. They were his first students.

Teacher of Compassion and the Causes of Suffering

After enlightenment, the Buddha spent the rest of his life teaching the principles of Buddhism—called the *Dharma,* or truth—until his death at the age of 80. The Buddha was not a god or a prophet, simply a man who taught from his own experience.

The Buddha taught that all life and existence involves suffering, pain and dissatisfaction. Even moments of happiness turn painful when the happiness is tightly held onto, captured or caged. He taught that in hopelessly trying to recreate the pleasures of the past, and in fruitlessly worrying about the uncertain future, life in-the-moment is missed.

> ## Words from the Wise
> *"He gave expression to truths of everlasting value and advanced the ethics not of India alone but of humanity. Buddha was one of the greatest ethical men of genius ever bestowed upon the world."*
> Dr. Albert Schweitzer, 1875-1965, Nobel Prize-winning surgeon and theologian

Followers of the Buddha's teachings helped make Buddhism the religion of India not long after his death. The king of India adopted a state philosophy of non-violence. Centuries later in India, Buddhism was replaced by Hinduism, the religion it had displaced. Around the same time that Jesus Christ lived and taught about peace and salvation in Nazareth and Jerusalem, Buddhism's message was spreading from India into Sri Lanka. Taking hundreds of years to spread from country to country, Buddhism was slowly adopted in Southeast Asia, Central Asia, China, Tibet and Japan.

The Noble Truths and Other Teachings

The Buddha called his teachings the Noble Truths. The way to peace and happiness, he taught, is through the acceptance of these Four Noble Truths:

1. Life involves suffering and dissatisfaction.
2. Suffering and dissatisfaction occur because of wanting life to be different than it is.
3. There is a way to become satisfied and achieve peace of mind.
4. This way requires following The Eightfold Noble Path.

The Buddha's Eightfold Noble Path are:

1) Right world view or understanding: See the world as it is, without assigning good or bad labels.

2) Right intention or aspiration: Think and make plans in a way that is neither too idealistic nor too materialistic.

3) Right speech: Tell the truth. Don't lie. Speak gently.

4) Right action: Respond appropriately to situations. Be aware of emotional influences to your actions.

5) Right livelihood: Earn money in a good way.

6) Right effort: Strive for balance and harmony.

7) Right mindfulness or awareness: Keep your mind calm and uncluttered.

8) Right concentration or meditation: Strike a thoughtful balance between relaxation and intensity.

Shortly before the Buddha's death he boiled down the Eight-fold Noble Path to three recommendations:

1) Want little.
2) Learn how to be satisfied.
3) Enjoy peace and tranquility.

Japan's Addition: The Sixteen Precepts

Buddhism slowly but steadily moved from India to China to Japan. In China, Buddhism was adopted by philosophical Taoists, who enjoyed the similarities between the Indian religion and Taoism's focus on human balance with nature. The result was a new philosophy called *Ch'an*, which when introduced to Japan became Zen. (In Korea, Zen is called *Son*.)

In Japan, the Buddha's teachings were folded into a set of moral codes of conduct called precepts. The monks who lived in Japanese monasteries studied the essence of *Buddha-nature* and condensed hundreds of early precepts into the sixteen of today. The sixteen precepts are broken into three groups, the first of which is called *The Three Refuges* or *The Three Treasures*:

1) I take refuge in the *Buddha* (translated from Sanskrit: 'awakened one')

   Not the worship of a person, but the learning about—and application of—being awake and being free from illusions.

2) I take refuge in the *Dharma* (translated from Sanskrit: 'law')

   The study and application of the Buddha's teachings.

3) I take refuge in the *Sangha* (translated from Sanskrit: 'community')

   Relating to others, meditating together, and experiencing the connection between nature, mankind and all living things.

The next group in the sixteen precepts is called *The Three Pure Precepts*:

1) Cease from evil

   Don't cause problems for yourself and others by acting on self-centered desires.

2) Do only good

   Focus on actions that help the world.

3) Do good for others

   Consider life—yours and others'—as not separate, and honor this sameness.

Rounding out the sixteen precepts are the *Ten Grave Precepts*. These are not commandments that if broken are considered sin, but a set of moral guidelines that when practiced will seem natural and effortless. The Ten Grave Precepts are:

1) I vow to refrain from killing.
2) I vow to refrain from stealing.
3) I vow to refrain from sexual misconduct and greed.
4) I vow to refrain from telling lies.
5) I vow to refrain from being intoxicated and being ignorant.
6) I vow to refrain from talking about others' errors and faults.
7) I vow to refrain from elevating myself and blaming others.
8) I vow to refrain from being selfish with money.
9) I vow to refrain from indulging in anger and hatred.
10) I vow to refrain from speaking ill of the Buddha, his teachings and the community.

The Three Characteristics of Life

Three pearls of wisdom that Zen teaches are early Buddhist doctrines called *The Three Dharma Seals of Excellence*, or *The Three Characteristics of Life*.

1) Impermanence

All living things are born or created, they grow old, and they die. This universal truth is fought and denied daily. Youth is revered and old age is feared. Death is seldom thought about, and almost never welcomed. The most precious moments of life are transitory, as are the worst. Everything changes constantly. Nothing remains the same. Acceptance of this impermanence is crucial to finding peace. Living in-the-moment as much as possible is the key.

2) Suffering

Everyone suffers in life, some more than others. For some, suffering is lack of food, water and shelter. For others, it is the inability to purchase a particular luxury item, or the presence of a pimple discovered just before arriving at a party. Whether physically or emotionally caused, suffering is omnipresent. While desire for suffering is ill-advised, acceptance of suffering as a part of life is a step toward self-awareness.

3) No-Self

It's convenient to see yourself through labels…salesperson, parent, motorcyclist, European. Labels, however, describe only elements of the individual, not the true entirety. Eliminate labels and descriptors of yourself and others, and you will see yourself as indefinable, as a blank sheet of paper onto which life may creatively draw.

Lessons from a Zen Sage

Around the year 1900 a university professor from the West visited Zen master Nan-in to learn about Zen. Nan-in poured tea into the professor's cup, but when the cup was full he kept pouring. The tea spilled on the floor. When the professor cried, *"Stop! It's full!"* Nan-in said, *"You are like this cup…too full. Only when you empty yourself of all opinions can you receive Zen."*

Zen's Roots in Chinese Taoism

It took centuries for Buddhism — and later, its offshoot Zen — to travel from country to country, culture to culture. With each new region, the teachings took on a local flavor, forever altering the messages taught.

Appendix A: The Story Behind Zen

Five hundred years after the Buddha died, his teachings made it to China. They were readily absorbed into Chinese culture because of their similarity to philosophical Taoism, which also taught harmony between man and nature, introspection and compassionate wisdom. Chinese Taoists were split into two schools of thought. One was religious and shamanistic, and one was more contemplative and philosophical.

Chinese preferring religious doctrine, perhaps tired of the distracting elements of mysticism and alchemy in religious Taoism, switched in great numbers to Buddhism. This became Mahayana Buddhism.

Chinese preferring philosophical doctrine appreciated Buddhism's Taoist-compatible views about earthly attachments and desires causing mankind's suffering. That merger created a practical, quasi-transcendentalist philosophy that advocated inner freedom and spontaneity. It was called *Ch'an*, from the Sanskrit *dhyana*, meaning meditation. Later, when Ch'an made its way into Japan, it was called Zen. The Japanese infused Zen with their own cultural beliefs, as have modern Westerners with theirs.

Taoism, the Zen-like philosophy of China, evolved through hundreds of years from the prehistoric practices of shamans, to the mystical *I Ching* (Book of Changes), to the study of the teachings of Lao Tzu and Chuang Tzu. Many debate whether either Taoist sage (master) was one writer, or a committee. Regardless, Lao Tzu's oral teachings—later recorded in the famous 5000 character, 81 chapter *Tao Te Ching*—and Chuang Tzu's teachings combined to create the basis of the Taoism that was prevalent when the Buddha's teachings arrived in China.

Taoism is as enigmatic and as indescribable as Zen. According to the Tao Te Ching, trying to define Taoism with words is impossible. It states, "The Tao that can be spoken of is not the real Way."

Taoism seeks to unite all things. Duality without balance, it teaches, prevents living in healthy wholeness. The words *Yin* and *Yang* come from Taoism, referring to the countering balances within nature, including birth and death, male and female, light and dark, summer and winter.

Following the Taoist tradition, speaking or writing about enlightenment is done infrequently within Zen. Enlightenment cannot be adequately described with mere words.

Zen, the philosophy, has similarities to, but is not the same thing as, Zen Buddhism, the religion. Zen Buddhism is part of the Mahayana school of Buddhism. The two other major schools of Buddhism are Theravada and Vajrayana.

Zen's Japanese Roots

Zen Buddhism in Japan has two primary sects: *Rinzai* and *Soto*.

Rinzai Zen, the *southern school*, teaches the possibility of instant enlightenment through the contemplation of *koans*, or enigmatic questions issued from master to student. The student considers what is the most Zen-like (simplest) answer. The famous *Genjo Koan* asks, "What is life all about?" The ultimate answer is "Look inside!"

Soto Zen, the *northern school*, teaches that enlightenment comes gradually, through sitting contemplatively in meditation.

The Buddha's teachings were accepted in Japan in the 9th century CE. Buddhism became the state religion of Japan during the Tokugawa era (1600-1868). An unfortunate mixing of priesthood and feudal leadership developed, and by the time the Meiji era began (1868), many Japanese were resentful and railed against Buddhism. Shinto then became the official religion of Japan. Under Shinto, the emperor was worshipped as a god, and Zen teachings were changed to reflect an Imperialist slant, as opposed to the original Buddhist foundation. Samurai warriors in training were taught by Zen masters how to eliminate the *self* during combat and sword fighting. This was called *Bushido*.

The darkest times for Zen were during the late 1930s when Japan invaded China and millions of Chinese, including women and children, were tortured and killed. At the time, Japanese anti-war protesters were executed. Some Zen priests, rather than risking their lives and holding firm to the non-violent teachings of the Buddha, gave encouragement and comfort to soldiers and generals. The Soto school of Japanese Zen has since issued a formal apology, yet it remains a sore spot among Zen practitioners that such an aberration in principles occurred.

Both Japanese Zen sects are active today. Soto has approximately three times as many followers as Rinzai.

Zen at Work

Over the centuries, Zen has evolved in its approach to work. The first Zen monks were ascetics who begged for food as they wandered from village to village pondering enlightenment. Later, Zen coalesced into a monastery-based, self-sufficient group of farming communities. Around 800 CE Zen master Pai-chang said, "If one does not work for a day, one should not eat for a day." It is said that when he became old and frail his followers hid his tools so he would not hurt himself working in the garden. Master Pai-chang went on a hunger strike until his tools were returned.

Monastic Zen life saw work take its place alongside meditation as a vehicle for self-awareness. Another Zen master, Hakuin, said, "For penetrating the depths of our true nature, nothing can surpass meditation during activity."

Modern World, Modern Zen

As of this writing, over 600 million people practice Buddhism worldwide, with 5 million of those in the United States. According to one recent study, approximately half of American Buddhists have graduate degrees.

When counting those who solely practice non-religious philosophies of Zen, the number reaches one billion practitioners worldwide. Add to that the people who principally call themselves Christians, Jews, Muslims or followers of other religions, but who also incorporate Zen principles in their life, and the number grows even higher.

In the United States there are more than a thousand Buddhist centers and more than a hundred Zen centers. These centers doubled in number between the years 1985 and 2003.

It took awhile for Zen to take hold in America. The three primary problems, dating from the mid-1800s, were:

1) American whites saw Eastern philosophy as racially impure and not fitting.
2) Americans considered the pursuit of science and technology superior to the pursuit of alternative spirituality.
3) Americans saw their religions as exclusive of, and superior to, Eastern philosophies.

As black jazz music gained white acceptance in the 1950s, an openness to the practices of other cultures developed. American beatniks and hippies, with their counterculture focus, adopted Zen practices such as meditation. Alan Watts and other intellectuals led the way.

In 1959 a Japanese Zen priest named Shunryu Suzuki arrived in San Francisco to run a small Zen center. It was a three-year assignment, but Suzuki stayed on until his death in 1971. The impact that the diminutive, unassuming Zen master had on those he taught in the San Francisco Zen Center, rippled outward across America. Suzuki's book, *Zen Mind, Beginner's Mind*, continues to be a bestseller.

The number of American Zen practitioners remained relatively low until the early 1990s. Society then paid attention to high-profile individuals such as the Dalai Lama (the exiled spiritual leader of Tibet), and to the practices of celebrities such as Richard Gere, Harrison Ford, John Cleese and Tina Turner. The public's increasing thirst for more information about Zen is being quenched by new Zen centers, periodicals, and the Internet — all of which combine to aid mutual appreciation and cross-cultural learning between East and West.

To delve deeper into Zen first requires reflection about what you wish to attain, and what you are willing to sacrifice for that attainment. For those focused on Zen Buddhism, the way of Zen is best learned through devoted study underneath a Zen master who has received *dharma transmission* (formal qualification to teach) from an earlier master, or *roshi*. Zen centers throughout the world provide this teaching. For those focused on non-religious, philosophical Zen, a combination of formal study and informal or self-study may work best. Although it's possible for someone entirely self-taught to have a keen Zen mind, the selective use of mentoring and instruction has obvious benefits.

Zen and Christianity

The third hindrance to Zen's early adoption in America was the view of Christianity as superior to, and exclusive of, other philosophies. This viewpoint has been eloquently addressed and challenged by experts such as Father Robert E. Kennedy, Ph.D., a Jesuit priest, a Zen Master and a practicing psychotherapist. His first book, *Zen Spirit, Christian Spirit* (1996), outlined how Zen fits neatly in the Christian life. Kennedy explained that Zen is a devotional form that may be useful to Christians.

His most recent book, *Zen Gifts to Christians* (2001), goes deeper into the spiritual life of Christians who use Zen. Kennedy describes how quiet meditation highlights a Christian's openness to new learning.[17]

Kim Boykin's book, *Zen for Christians: A Beginner's Guide*, published in 2003, emphasizes such things as breath control and increased thought awareness in a collection of techniques designed to help those of the Christian faith.[18]

Zen and Judaism

In his book, *One God Clapping: The Spiritual Path of a Zen Rabbi*, published in 1999, rabbi Alan Lew explains the Jewish meditation movement, and how the merger of two ancient traditions helps everyday life. Told through a series of stories, Lew's book uncovers revealing instructions that assist in Jewish spiritual growth.[19]

The Future of Zen

Zen has adapted itself to each culture that has welcomed it over the last two millennia. The trend continues. The Western world is seeing a modernized Zen that appeals to many, while still maintaining the ancient teachings and wisdom. In the hectic world of business and sales, Zen's lessons remain timeless and useful. The approachability of Zen is a direct result of its:

- Inclusive openness to anyone, of any religious or philosophical background

- Intellectual slant that is open to skepticism, self-examination and modification.

Future generations will know an even different Zen, one that fits their world. Yet the mindful lessons of awareness, balance, compassion, beginner's mind and reduction of suffering through the examination of desire will touch human nature forever.

We shall not cease from exploration
And at the end of all our exploring
Will be to arrive where we started
And know the place for the first time
- T. S. Eliot

APPENDIX B:
ZEN RESOURCES

The Best Early Books About Zen

- *An Introduction to Zen Buddhism* by D.T. Suzuki, 1952
- *Beat Zen, Square Zen and Zen* by Alan Watts, 1959
- *Zen Flesh, Zen Bones: A Collection of Zen and Pre-Zen Writings* by Paul Reps, 1960
- *The Way of Zen* by Alan Watts, 1965
- *Manual of Zen Buddhism* by D.T. Suzuki, 1969
- *Zen Buddhism and Psychoanalysis* by Erich Fromm, 1970
- *Zen Mind, Beginner's Mind* by Shunryu Suzuki, 1970
- *Zen in the Art of Archery* by Eugene Herrigel, 1971
- *A Primer of Soto Zen: A Translation of Dogen's Shobogenzo Zuimonki* by Eihei Dogen 1971
- *Zen: A Way of Life* by Christmas Humphreys, 1971
- *A Western Approach to Zen* by Christmas Humphreys,1972
- *The Essentials of Zen Buddhism* by D.T. Suzuki, 1973
- *This Is It* by Alan Watts, 1973
- *Zen of Seeing* by Frederick Franck, 1973
- *Zen and the Art of Motorcycle Maintenance: An Inquiry into Values* by Robert M. Pirsig, 1974
- *The Method of Zen* by Eugene Herrigel, 1974
- *Zen Philosophy, Zen Practice* by Thich Thien-An, 1975
- *Games Zen Masters Play: The Writings of R. H. Blyth* by Robert Sohl, 1976
- *Zen Poems* by Thich Nhat Hanh, 1976

Other Excellent Books About Zen

- *Not Always So: Practicing the True Spirit of Zen* by Shunryu Suzuki, Edward Espe Brown (Editor)
- *The Three Pillars of Zen* by Roshi Philip Kapleau
- *Crooked Cucumber: The Life and Zen Teaching of Shunryu Suzuki* by David Chadwick
- *Tao Te Ching* by Gia-Fu Feng (Translator)
- Any book by Pema Chödrön

Partial List of U.S. Zen Centers

Alabama
- Green Mountain Zen Center www.gmzc.us

Alaska
- Cold Mountain Zen Center in Fairbanks Alaska
  www.geocities.com/coldmountainzencenter

Arizona
- Desert Lotus Zen Sangha www.vuu.org/zen
- Haku-un-ji Zen Center www.zenarizona.com

Arkansas
- Little Rock Zen Group www.geocities.com/arkansaszen

California
- Empty Gate Zen Center www.emptygatezen.com
- Zen Mountain Center www.zmc.org
- Santa Monica Zen Center www.smzc.org
- Del Mar Zen Center www.ttzc.org
- Berkeley Zen Center www.berkeleyzencenter.org
- Hazy Moon Zen Center www.hazymoon.com
- San Diego Zen Center www.sddharma.com
- San Francisco Zen Center www.sfzc.org

- Los Angeles Zen Center www.zencenter.org
- Los Angeles Dharma Zen Center www.dharmazen.com
- Mountain Spirit Center www.mountainspiritcenter.net
- Zen Mountain Monastery www.mro.org
- Ocean Eyes Zen Center www.oezc.com

Colorado
- Open Circle Zen Community www.opencirclezen.org
- Great Mountain Zen Center www.gmzc.org

Connecticut
- New Haven Zen Center www.newhavenzen.org

Delaware
- Delaware Valley Zen Center www.dvzc.com

Florida
- Cypress Tree Zen Group www.freenet.tlh.fl.us/~cypress
- Gateless Gate Zen Center www.gatelessgate.org

Georgia
- ZenSpace www.zenspace.org

Illinois
- Peoria Zen Center www.peoriazen.com
- Ten Directions Zen Community
  www.geocities.com/chicagozen

Indiana
- Indianapolis Zen Center www.indyzen.org

Kansas
- Kansas Zen Center in Lawrence www.kansaszencenter.org

Louisiana
- AZI New Orleans www.nozt.org

Maine
- Northern Light Zen Center www.cambridgezen.com/nlzc

Maryland
- Zen Community of Baltimore www.zcbclaresangha.org

Massachusetts
- Cambridge Zen Center www.cambridgezen.com

Milwaukee
- Great Lake Zen Center in Milwaukee www.glzc.org

Nevada
- Great Bright Zen Center www.greatbrightzen.homestead.com

New Hampshire
- Southern New Hampshire Zen Group www.nhzen.org

New York
- Chogye International Zen Center www.cizny.org

Pennsylvania
- Zen Group of Pittsburgh www.zengrouppitt.org

Rhode Island
- Providence Zen Center www.kwanumzen.org/pzc

Virginia
- Still Water Zen Center www.mindspring.com/~bellsound

Washington
- Dharma Sound Zen Center www.dharmasound.org

Wisconsin
- Isthmus Zen Community www.execpc.com/~magglpie

Partial List of Worldwide Zen Centers

Australia
- Queensland Zen Centre in Australia
  www.members.optushome.com.au/qldzen

Austria
- Vienna Zen Center www.kwanumzen.at.tt

Brazil
- Modesto Grupo deMeditadores
  www.geocities.com/umgm594

China
- Su Bong Zen Monastery (HK) www.subong.org.hk

Czech Republic
- Prague Zen Centre www.kwanumzen.cz

France
- Paris Zen Center www.pariszencenter.com
- Association Zen Internationale (AZI) www.zen-azi.org

Germany
- Berlin Zen Center www.kwanumzen.de

Israel
- Dogen-Soto Zen Dojo www.zenki.com

Japan
- Gyokuryu-ji www.geocities.com/not_one_not_two
- Dogen Sangha www.dogensangha.org

Korea
- Mu Sang Sa International Zen Center www.musangsa.org

Lithuania
- Vilnius Zen Center www.zen.lt

Norway
- Norway Soto Zen Center www.sotozen.no

Poland
- Katowice Zen Group www.katowice.zen.pl
- Lódz Zen Center www.zen.insite.com.pl

Singapore
- Singapore Zen Center www.kyclzen.org

Spain
- Palma Zen Center in Spain www.mallorcaweb.net/zen

United Kingdom
- Bristol Ch'an Group www.bristol-chan.co.uk
- London Serene Meditation Group
    www.rptowen.co.uk/Serene.Reflection.London

Other Web Sites

- BuddhaNet www.buddhanet.net
- Tricycle www.tricycle.com
- Daily Zen www.dailyzen.com
- BeliefNet www.beliefnet.com
- DharmaNet www.dharma.net
- International Campaign for Tibet www.savetibet.org
- Robert Thurman www.spiritwalk.org/thurman.htm
- DharmaCrafts www.dharmacrafts.com
- Peacemaker Circles www.peacemakercircle.org
- Zen and Business www.zenandbusiness.org
- Zen Hospice Project www.zenhospice.org

NOTES AND BIBLIOGRAPHY

1. Alan Watts, *The Way of Zen*, 1957, New York Vintage Books, p77

2. Frank Salisbury, Cariona Neary and Karl O'Connor, *Coaching Champions: How to Get the Absolute Best Out of Your Salespeople*, 2002, Oak Tree Press

3. David Chadwick, *Crooked Cucumber*, 2000, Bantam Doubleday Dell

4. Kimberly A. Williams, Ph.D., West Virginia University in Morgantown, study published in *American Journal of Health Promotion*, 2001

5. Shunryu Suzuki, Zen master and founder of the San Francisco Zen Center, *Zen Mind, Beginner's Mind*, 1971, Weatherhill

6. Lisa van der Pool, *Follow-up is Number One with Buyers*, Purchasing Magazine, November 18, 1999, excerpted with permission

7. Ron S. Fortgang, David A. Lax and James K. Sebenius, *Negotiating the Spirit of the Deal, Harvard Business Review*, February 2003, excerpted with permission

8. Tom Hopkins, *How to Master the Art of Selling* , 1982, Warner Books

9. Lee Iacocca, *Iacocca: An Autobiography*, 1984, Bantam

10. Albert Mehrabian, Professor Emeritus of Psychology, UCLA, 1989

11. *Strategic Sales Presentations*, 1993, Shipley Associates

12. Robert Thurman, Ph.D., *Inner Revolution: Life, Liberty and the Pursuit of Real Happiness*, 1998, Riverhead Books

13. Anne Seibold Drapeau and Robert Galford, *The Enemies of Trust*, *Harvard Business Review*, Feb. 1, 2003, excerpted with permission

14. Gilbert A. Churchill Jr., and J. Paul Peter, 1998 study by conducted by Irwin / McGraw-Hill; information extracted from Dartnell Corporation's *1997 Sales Force Compensation Survey of Business-to-Business Salespeople*

15. Richard Carlson, Ph.D., *Don't Sweat the Small Stuff at Work*, 1998, Hyperion

16. Alain Morin, Ph.D., *On a Relation between Inner Speech and Self-Awareness: Additional Evidence from Brain Studies*, Mt. Royal College, Alberta, Canada, 1998

17. Fr. Robert E. Kennedy, S.J., Ph.D. Professor of Theology and Japanese at St. Peter's College, Jersey City; awarded title of *Roshi* (Zen Master) in 1997; awarded doctorates in Theology from the University of Ottawa and from St. Paul University in Ottawa

18. *Zen for Christians: A Beginner's Guide*, Kim Boykin, 2003, Jossey-Bass

19. Alan Lew is the rabbi of the conservative Congregation Beth Sholom in San Francisco. His work in using Zen meditation to enhance Jewish spirituality has been highlighted on *ABC News*, PBS's news magazine *Religion and Ethics*, and *The MacNeil-Lehrer Report*.

INDEX

Index

Running, 156
Russell, Bertrand, 151
Ryokan, 171

S

Sahn, Seung, 119
Sales 99, 61
Sales managers, 28
Sales meetings, 146
Sameness, 41, 106, 112, 150, 158
Samurai, 197
San Francisco Zen Center, 199
Sangha, 193
Schweitzer, Dr. Albert, 124, 191
Self confidence, 47
Self-absorption, 137
Self-discovery, 50
Selling journal, 179
Sex, 38
Shinto, 197
Single-tasking, 45
Six Perfections, 158
Sixteen Precepts, 192
Smiling, 111, 172
Socrates, 19, 99, 106, 114
Soto Zen, 197
Spam, 92, 94
Spirituality, 37
Statement of credibility. *See* Credibility
Storytelling, 106
Strategic Selling, 71
Strategy, 72, 98
Stress, 28, 30, 112, 152
Stretching, 155, 177
Success, 37
Suffering, 191, 195
Suzuki, Shunryu, 29, 42, 199
Sympathy, 66

T

Tao Te Ching, 196
Taoism, 16, 196

Team Presentation, 107
Teams, 141
Telephone Prospecting, 84
The 7 Habits of Highly Effective People, 12
Theravada Buddhism, 197
Thoreau, Henry David, 7
Three Characteristics of Life, 194
Thurman, Robert, Ph.D, 121
Time management, 135, 174
Transcendentalism, 157
Trust, 7, 45, 62, 64, 126
Trustworthiness, 28, 81

U

Uncertainty, 29

V

Vajrayana Buddhism, 197
Values, 17, 23, 27, 34, 39, 53, 65, 160
Videotaping, 105
Voice, 106
von Goethe, Johann Wolfgang, 123

W

Wall Street Journal, 125
Wanting, 158
Watts, Alan, 18, 199
Weight training, 55
Weiss, Laurie,Ph.D, 69
What-have-you-done-for-me-lately?, 176
Who Moved My Cheese?, 15
Why-I-work statement, 161
Wisdom, 37
Workload, 173
Workplace friendships, 133
Writing style, 92

Y

Yoga, 55, 155, 177